HarperCollins *practical gardener*

ARCHITECTURAL
PLANTS

CHRISTINE SHAW

HarperResource
An Imprint of HarperCollinsPublishers

DEDICATION

This book is for my Dad, Harry Shaw, who first showed me what a pleasure gardening can be, and also for Angus White, to thank him for his support and encouragement, and for introducing me to the world of architectural plants.

First published in Great Britain in 2003 by HarperCollins*Publishers* Ltd.

HARPERCOLLINS PRACTICAL GARDENER: ARCHITECTURAL PLANTS.
Text by Christine Shaw; copyright © 2003, 2004 HarperCollins*Publishers*.
Artworks and design copyright © 2003, 2004 HarperCollins*Publishers*.

Photography by Christine Shaw and Tim Sandall. For a detailed breakdown, see page 160.

Photographic props: Coolings Nurseries, Rushmore Hill, Knockholt, Kent, TN14 7NN, UK, www.coolings.co.uk

Design and Editorial: Focus Publishing, Sevenoaks, Kent, UK
Project Editor: Guy Croton
Project Coordinator: Caroline Watson
Design and Illustration: David Etherington
Assistant Editor: Vanessa Townsend

For HarperCollins*Publishers*:
Managing Editor: Angela Newton
Art Direction: Luke Griffin
Editor: Alastair Laing

ISBN 0-06-073337-3

Color reproduction by Colourscan
Printed and bound in Hong Kong by Printing Express Ltd.

Contents

Introduction   6
How to Use This Book   7

Assessing Your Garden   8
Choosing Plants   10
Planting   14
Care & Maintenance   16
Propagation   24
Planting Combinations   28

Bamboos & Grasses   32

Ferns & Palms   43

Climbers   52

Trees   61

Spiky & Succulent Plants   91

Other Leafy Exotics   106

Troubleshooting   152
Pests & Diseases   154

Index of Plants   158
General Index   159
Acknowledgments   160

Introduction

For a plant to be architectural, it has to have either a very strong shape or a very strong presence in the garden, and preferably throughout the year. Some plants such as agaves, yuccas, palms, and tree ferns have obvious architectural qualities: think of the spiky leaves of an agave bursting out of the ground; a palm's lush display of leaves like splayed fingers; or the fibrous texture of a tree fern trunk topped by a spreading crown of delicate fronds. Some, such as Arbutus, Eucalyptus, Pittosporum, and Phillyrea, are much more understated in what they have to offer, but all make themselves noticed for different reasons, whether for their beautiful bark, glossy or subtly colored leaves, or shapely outline when mature. Then there are the architectural plants that simply demand attention, such as bananas, paulownias, hedychiums, and cannas. These are the plants that make a bold, brash statement in the garden, adding a touch of glamor with their huge leaves or large, brilliantly-colored flowers. Above all, architectural plants are never boring!

The number of plants that could be considered "architectural" is in fact quite small, and this book offers you an introduction to 114 of the best and most commonly

The quintessentially architectural spike of Kniphofia

available varieties. Though the range to choose from is limited, a garden full of architectural plants can look incredible, and many different looks can be achieved—from a wild, steamy jungle to the more ornamental restraint of a Japanese garden. Having a garden full of architectural plants is very appealing, but they are versatile enough to be introduced into other types of garden in smaller numbers, to accent particular areas. However "normal" a garden may seem, adding just one large palm tree will provide an impressive feature without dominating the rest of the garden or looking out of place in its surroundings. Similarly, a water feature that seems somehow lacking in presence in the garden, will be considerably enlivened with the introduction of a group of bamboos.

The demand for architectural plants has been steadily increasing over the past ten years and they are now enjoying a massive wave of popularity that shows no sign of slowing down. In fact, this type of gardening is the fastest growing area of horticulture, as more and more gardeners realize, often with great relief, that there is an alternative to herbaceous borders and rose bushes. More and more people are becoming devoted to the idea of growing something exotic in their garden. Whether it is just one or two plants, or a garden full of them, their popularity continues to soar. Yet although information on palms, yuccas, cordylines, phormiums, and tree ferns is becoming more widespread, it can still be difficult to obtain comprehensive advice. This book sets out to provide all that you will need—so that you can enjoy these truly amazing plants in their full glory.

Architectural plants will enhance any kind of garden or building

How to Use This Book

The book is divided into three parts. The opening chapters guide you through all areas of garden practice, from assessing your site, through planting and general care, to propagation techniques. A comprehensive plant directory follows, with individual entries on nearly 120 of the most commonly available architectural plants, listed in alphabetical order, with separate chapters on ferns and palms, climbers, trees, spiky and succulent plants, and other leafy exotics. The final section of the book covers plant problems. Troubleshooting pages allow you to diagnose the likely cause of any problems, and a directory of pests and diseases offers advice on how to solve them.

latin name of the plant genus, followed by its **common name**

hardiness symbols denote a plant's degree of hardiness

alphabetical tabs on the side of the page, color-coded to help you quickly find the plant you want

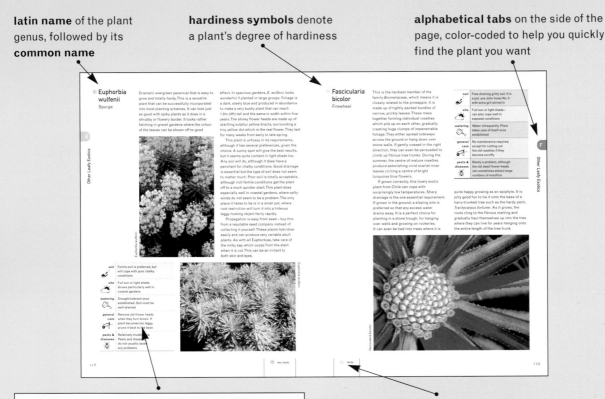

care tables list the growing requirements of each plant in note form for quick reference, covering:

 soil
   the best soil for growing in terms of nutrients, drainage, and chemical content

 site
   whether to plant in a sunny, shady, or part-shaded position, and the degree of shelter required

 watering
   essential information on the watering requirements of each plant

 general care
   tips on feeding, mulching, watering, support, etc.

 pests & diseases
   whether the plant is prone to any particular problems and how to treat them

a key at the bottom of the page explains what each symbol means

hardiness symbols indicate a plant's degree of hardiness in terms of the temperatures it will withstand:

❄ **very hardy**
a plant listed as being "very hardy" will withstand even the most extreme weather conditions (to -4°F)

❄ **hardy**
a plant listed as being "hardy" will withstand all but the most extreme weather conditions, including temperatures as low as 14°F

❄ **tender**
a plant listed as being "tender" will require winter protection in all but the mildest climates, withstanding temperatures to 25°F

Assessing Your Garden

Before paying a visit to the garden center or nursery, it is important to spend some time assessing the type of garden you have, so that you can make an informed choice when selecting your architectural plants.

Sun or shade?

The notes on cultivation that accompany each plant featured in this book include reference to the best place to grow them in the garden, according to the amount of sun they require. If your garden is in full sun throughout most of the day, there is little point in trying to grow ferns and fatsias. Similarly, if your garden is in shade all day, trying to grow desert plants such as agaves would give very disappointing results. However, if your garden is shady for, say, half the day, then you should be able to grow plants that prefer a semi-shady aspect or full shade, alongside the sun-loving varieties.

Architectural plants are many and varied, but all have their own specific needs.

Moisture content

After a heavy spell of rain, take a walk around the garden to see which areas are retaining water and which dry out fairly quickly, and whether or not there is good drainage overall. If your garden is always soggy, then it is a good idea to choose plants such as bamboos, bananas, gunneras, and cannas, which thrive in such conditions. However, if the ground is always dry and inhospitable, stick to growing plants such as yuccas, agaves, Arbutus, and Phillyrea. In reality, most gardens have different conditions throughout. There is always one part that dries out the quickest and always one part that remains wetter than the rest. Most gardens, therefore, can grow quite a wide variety of all types of plant.

Increasing the moisture content of the soil manually is always an option, but the need for constant watering can become very labor intensive and requires a strong will.

Soil

The two most important things to find out when first assessing the soil in your garden is whether it is acid or alkaline and what level of fertility it has to offer. Alkaline soil has a high lime content and some plants do not perform well in this type of soil. Kits are available from most garden centers to test for alkalinity.

Soil fertility is one area where growing conditions can definitely be altered. Although some plants need virtually no nutrients, other plants are very greedy indeed. If your choice of plants includes palms or bamboos and your soil is not the most nutritious, then annual feeding with a concentrated fertilizer is essential.

Exposure

Another factor to consider is how much your garden is exposed to, or sheltered from, the wind. If you live on the coast or on the top of a hill, strong winds will probably be a regular feature. Although some plants such as Baccharis, *Quercus ilex*, and Dasylirion can easily cope, many cannot. Bamboos will develop brown edges to their leaves and large-leafed plants such as Paulownia and bananas will have a permanently shabby appearance with torn and shredded foliage. If yours is a garden with a walled courtyard in a sheltered city, then the range of plants you can choose is much greater. In fact, virtually anything will grow in such conditions. As a rough guide, the larger the leaves of the plant, the less likely it will be able to cope with strong gales.

Specific Conditions

Each garden is different, with its own specific, prevailing conditions to take into account. The illustration below is a representation of a "typical" garden, comprising different elements that usually feature in most gardens.

Of course, your own garden may look very different from the one illustrated here, but you will almost certainly need to take the same factors into account when assessing the suitability of your garden for the cultivation of architectural plants. Remember that it is always easier to work with conditions as you find them. Don't try too hard to fight Nature, because Nature usually wins in the end. That said, with a few slight changes to your garden, you can improve considerably your plants' chances of growing, without too much effort and expense.

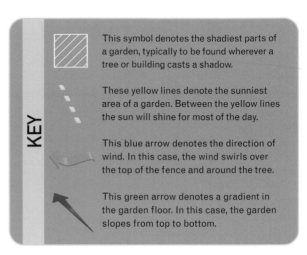

KEY

This symbol denotes the shadiest parts of a garden, typically to be found wherever a tree or building casts a shadow.

These yellow lines denote the sunniest area of a garden. Between the yellow lines the sun will shine for most of the day.

This blue arrow denotes the direction of wind. In this case, the wind swirls over the top of the fence and around the tree.

This green arrow denotes a gradient in the garden floor. In this case, the garden slopes from top to bottom.

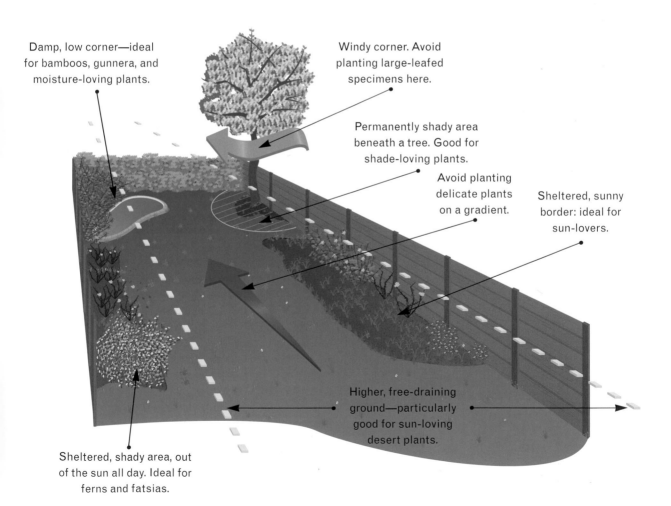

Damp, low corner—ideal for bamboos, gunnera, and moisture-loving plants.

Windy corner. Avoid planting large-leafed specimens here.

Permanently shady area beneath a tree. Good for shade-loving plants.

Avoid planting delicate plants on a gradient.

Sheltered, sunny border: ideal for sun-lovers.

Sheltered, shady area, out of the sun all day. Ideal for ferns and fatsias.

Higher, free-draining ground—particularly good for sun-loving desert plants.

Choosing Plants

When it comes to buying plants, knowing what type of garden you have in terms of shade, sun, available moisture, soil pH, and fertility will help you to choose plants tailored to your needs. However, there are a few other considerations that require a bit of thought. Do you want to create an instantaneous effect or are you prepared to wait? Do you have a lot of time or would you prefer a garden that requires minimal effort? Are you creating a garden with containers or incorporating containers into the overall design?

Initial impact

If you are the type of gardener who likes to watch plants grow, then you will be able to save money by choosing tiny seedlings, and gain satisfaction from nurturing the plants through to maturity. However, you must be prepared to wait several years for your garden to take shape. And there is always the danger when buying very small plants that you will be tempted to plant them too close together to try and create some semblance of lush verdancy. This is fine for a few years, but gradually, as the plants grow, more and more will have to be thinned out and either distributed among your other gardening friends, or simply disposed of. Ideally, they should all be planted with their eventual size in mind. The gaps between each tiny plant could be filled temporarily with rocks, decorative mulch or plants in terracotta pots.

Plant *Dicksonia antarctica* to make an instant, bold statement.

On the other hand, if you are the type of gardener who wants to create an instantly impressive display, then you will need to buy more mature specimens, which, since the garden center or nursery has spent time and money nurturing them, are bound to be more expensive. Yet planting to create an instant impact is much easier and less time-consuming than starting from scratch. It can also be great fun with rewarding results from day one.

Maintenance

The kind of life you lead should have a direct bearing on the type of garden to aim for. If you have plenty of free time to lavish on your garden, then you need not hold back from growing some of the trickier plants that demand regular attention throughout the year to flourish. If, however, you lead a busy life that prohibits lengthy spells in the garden, choosing low-maintenance plants is vital. You should avoid those plants upon which you simply could not spend the time needed to nurture them to full glory. This doesn't mean your garden has to be dull—far from it! Here are just a fraction of the lovely yet virtually maintenance-free plants, you could choose from: palm trees (*Trachycarpus fortunei*), strawberry trees (*Arbutus* x *andrachnoides*), yuccas, dwarf palms (*Chamaerops humilis*), sempervivums, and creeping rosemary (*Rosmarinus repens*).

Agaves are generally low maintenance and easy to keep healthy.

Plants in Containers

Why grow plants in pots?

If your patch of garden consists of a balcony, roof terrace, or paved courtyard, then growing plants in containers is your best option. Pots are also useful for quickly filling bare patches in the garden, or creating temporary interest in the spaces between young plants that have yet to mature. Putting a plant in a container is also a useful way of making it stand out and appear more impressive than if it were simply planted in the ground.

Choosing the correct container

The traditional flowerpot is a carefully chosen shape. The fact that it is wide at the top, narrow at the bottom, and has smooth, straight sides means that however pot-bound a plant becomes, it can always be pulled out. Although there are some beautifully-shaped creations available, pots with extravagantly curved sides and narrow tops should only be used as ornaments for the garden. Otherwise, when the plant needs to be moved into something larger, the only options are to smash the pot or chop off some of the plant's root system.

Selecting suitable plants for pots

There are two categories of architectural plants that are successfully grown in containers. Firstly, plants that are very slow-growing such as *Chamaerops humilis*,

Always choose pots that are wider at the top than the base.

Slow-growing plants are ideal for containers.

> **TIP**
> Containers are unnatural environments for plants, so keeping them healthy is not that easy. Ensure that there is good drainage—lots of broken crocks in the bottom and a large drainage hole. Don't keep the plant cramped up in a small pot, which causes added stress. Water regularly—lack of water is the most important cause of failure.

Trochodendron aralioides, *Dicksonia antarctica*, *Libertia formosa*, *Aloe aristata*, and *Echeveria glauca*. Secondly, desert plants, which are adept at coping with long periods of drought, burning hot sun during the day, and freezing cold temperatures at night. Try *Yucca aloifolia*, Dasylirions, and all types of agaves.

Buying Plants

Where to buy from

There are two main choices when it comes to buying plants: specialist nurseries or garden centers. Up until about ten years ago, few people had heard of the expression "architectural plants." It was very unusual to see cordylines, phormiums, palms, and hardy bananas for sale anywhere. Since then, the demand for hardy exotics has soared. Their popularity is still very much on the increase and many garden centers are beginning to latch onto this phenomenon. They still have a long way to go, but garden centers are definitely becoming more adventurous, and many are well worth checking out.

Nurseries

Specialist nurseries are the backbone of the horticultural establishment and, since many of them struggle against the odds, they deserve as much support as they can get from the plant-buying public.

There are many advantages to buying architectural plants from a specialist nursery, starting with the sheer range of plants on offer. Many nurseries specialize in cultivating a single group of plants, selling just bamboos or palms or ferns. They not only offer a wide variety of plants in their chosen specialist area, but can also back this up with expert knowledge and advice on how to care for them. Many nurseries sell their produce directly to the public, so there's no middle man to take his cut. As such, the plants are usually extremely good value for money. Nurseries specializing in architectural plants often have a wide range of sizes available. As the number of plants

Watch out for weed-ridden plants.

> ### WHAT TO AVOID
>
> **Horticultural establishments are variable in the quality of their produce. Just because it's a nursery doesn't mean that all will be well. Similarly, just because it's a garden center doesn't mean that specimens will be less healthy. Common sense must prevail, and plants with any of the following traits should be left on the shelf.**
>
> 1. Small, undersized foliage
>
> 2. Leaves that are brown, yellow, or shriveled
>
> 3. Masses of roots hanging out of the bottom of the pot.
>
> 4. No sign of any roots at all.
>
> 5. Considerable leaf-drop
>
> 6. A pot so weed-ridden that the plant can only just be detected.
>
> 7. Pots containing completely dry potting soil that clearly hasn't been watered for a very long time.
>
> The perfect specimen should be weed-free, have been recently watered and, most importantly, should have leaves that are bursting with health, with a few roots showing at the bottom.

A specialist nursery can be an inspiration.

classed as "architectural" run to the hundreds, rather than thousands, stockists have the freedom to offer fewer types of plants but in a whole range of sizes. For example, a nursery specializing in palms would be able to offer plants from just a few inches high through to mature specimens 20ft (6m) tall.

In addition, nurseries are usually fascinating places to visit in their own right. If you are a novice gardener, seeing so many weird and wonderful varieties in one place, and hearing experts talk with such passion about

their subject, can be an inspirational experience. And if you are already an experienced gardener, it's always pleasant to be in the company of other people who share your particular (or peculiar) interest—where else could you go and chat for three hours about the "clustered node bases" of bamboos?

Garden centers

Advantages to buying architectural plants from garden centers, assuming they are adventurous enough to stock such things, are, first of all, the convenience. They are a feature of most towns, and many people live only a short distance away from one. Garden centers also stock a huge range of sundries. Here is a place where you can buy bags of potting mix, mulch, garden tools, terracotta pots, trellis, plant food, hose pipes, insecticides, and just about everything else you can think of. Hence plants may not always be at the top of their agenda, but if you can find one that sells all these sundries and even a few of the architectural plants on your wish list, then you have found a good one.

Specialist nurseries can be spectacular places to visit.

Small Eucalyptus plants rapidly grow into large trees.

The Cost

Maturity

Getting to know how quickly plants reach maturity will help you to plan your expenditure. If you wish to purchase Eucalyptus, for example, these trees are so fast-growing that to spend money on a large plant is almost pointless. On the other hand, palms are painfully slow-growing and to buy a very small plant, hoping to have it as the centerpiece of your garden one day, is a real long-term project and could be frustrating until it happens. Generally, if a plant is reasonably priced, that tends to mean it is fairly fast-growing, and plants that seem expensive are usually slow-growing.

Size and hardiness

Something else to consider before working out a budget is the size of a plant in relation to its hardiness. For example, desert-type plants such as agaves can cope with cold, wet winters much more successfully if they are at least 2ft (60cm) tall. As a general rule, it might be worth spending a little extra money on a more mature plant in the long run, if a younger, cheaper plant is less likely to withstand the conditions in your garden.

Planting

Preparing the soil

Before planting anything, it is vital to prepare the soil so that the plants will enjoy adequate amounts of nutrition, moisture, and drainage.

Check that the soil is fertile enough to support what you intend growing there. If selected plants need rich soil and yours is lacking in vitality, prepare the planting site thoroughly by digging in well-rotted manure or plenty of blood, fish, and bone.

Next, check that the soil has the correct moisture content. If the soil is too dry, make sure that a tap is close by so that watering isn't too much of a chore. Alternatively, consider installing automatic irrigation. If the soil is too wet for the plants chosen, dig over the site first and incorporate as much grit, rubble, or gravel as you can so that excess rain does not settle around the roots, but drains away.

Dig plenty of grit into the soil to help with drainage.

Planting into the Ground

It is important to plant trees, shrubs, and herbaceous plants at the correct depth into the soil. The amount of root under the ground must be exactly the same as when the plant was in its pot. If a plant is placed too low, water can settle into the crown (the central growth point) of the plant, which could lead to rotting. If a plant is placed too high, surface roots could be left exposed to the air. These will then dry out quickly and die.

Planting a tree

Trees should be planted with more care than any other plant and, since most do not like being transplanted, the position chosen should be regarded as permanent. Although bare-rooted trees are still sold, most trees sold nowadays are container-grown. The method for planting is as follows:

Gently remove the young tree from its container, taking care not to damage the rootball. Dig a hole slightly larger than the container [A], using the empty pot as a measuring guide [B]. Loosen up any compacted soil at the bottom of the hole to help with drainage as the tree's roots become established in the soil.

Sprinkle in a handful of bonemeal. This provides a boost of nutrition to help the roots get off to a good start. Gently place the tree in the hole, ensuring that the tree is standing straight. Check that the old planting level of the tree matches its new one, i.e. the top of the potting mix around the roots is exactly level to the top of the planting hole. Carefully replace the soil in the hole and firm it all down gently [C]. Take three 6ft (1.8m) stakes

A well-staked tree is less prone to damage by wind.

arrangement makes it more difficult to damage the tree with lawnmowers or through vandalism.

Planting other plants

The technique for a plant is similar to that for trees, but there is usually no need to provide supporting stakes. Dig a hole slightly greater in volume than the plant's container, loosening any compacted soil at the base so that the roots are not prevented from spreading. If you are planting a desert plant that prefers dry, free-draining soil, add a thin layer of grit at the bottom of the hole; for all other plants add bonemeal to provide extra nutrition for the roots. Position the plant and replace the soil.

Mulching

When planting is complete, particularly if you have planted up large areas of the garden, consider mulching all around your new plants. Mulching is the term used for spreading thick layers of suitable material on top of the soil, such as colored gravel, pebbles, or chipped bark.

This is done for several reasons: to highlight the plants; to keep the moisture content of the soil high by eliminating evaporation; and, if applied in layers of at least 3in (7cm) thick, to help prevent weeds. Applying an organic mulch will also work wonders on soil texture, improving the water retention of lighter soils and lightening heavy soils so that they drain more easily.

and tie kits, and hammer them 2ft (60cm) into the ground 120° apart around the tree [D]. Using three stakes ensures that a) nothing is hammered through the root area, b) whatever direction the wind is blowing, the bark will never rub against the stakes (*see above*), c) this

Planting in Containers

With the exception of tree ferns, the same soil mix can be used for all plants growing in containers. Use a good-quality, soil-based potting mix, plus up to 50% extra grit stirred in. The addition of grit makes for a rich, fertile mixture that is also free-draining, which eliminates the hunt around the garden searching for large stones or chunks of smashed pots to line the base of the container.

A good quality soil-based potting mix has a number of advantages over a soilless mix. It contains enough food to nourish the plants for many weeks; it is heavier than a soilless mix, so containers are less likely

to blow over in the wind; and it can be rehydrated more easily if allowed to dry out. Tree ferns require a potting mix based on a peat substitute, with some leaf mold added, if you can obtain it.

Below is a *Yucca floribunda* being replanted into a larger container. Position the plant and add a good soil-based potting mix with added grit [A]. Fill the container to just below the rim [B] and then finish off with a layer of gravel on top of the potting mix to prevent it from drying out [C].

A

B

C

Care & Maintenance

All plants need a little care and attention if they are to thrive. Simple maintenance, as outlined here, will help to ensure a fantastic garden year-round.

Feeding

Specific feeding requirements for each individual plant are provided in the directory section of the book, but here are some general tips on feeding plants that will make your life easier and your plants healthier.

When to feed

Plants can only absorb food when they are actively growing. This is usually, but by no means always, during the spring. As such, if you are feeding each plant individually, this will mainly need to be done between mid-spring and mid-summer. Throwing food at a plant when it is dormant is pointless.

If you are creating whole new areas in the garden, then it makes sense to incorporate food when all the heavy digging and preparation is being done, which is often during the fall so that planting can begin early the following year.

Canna indica enjoys a liquid feed.

What to use

All gardeners tend to have their favorite plant food, which they feel best caters for the needs of their garden and their plants. Whatever fertilizer is chosen, provided that the instructions on the packet are followed exactly, more or less any feed is better than no feed at all. Knowing the main constituents, and understanding how each chemical benefits a particular area of the plant, will help determine your choice of fertilizer (*see box below*).

If you are preparing large areas of the garden, sprinkling a proprietary brand of concentrated farmyard manure over the surface of the dug-over soil several weeks before you start planting is highly recommended. Manure not only boosts the level of nutrients in the soil, but also improves the overall structure and water content of the soil, and encourages earthworms with their beneficial effect on soil quality. Most importantly, however, you will have the lovely smell of the farmyard wafting around the entire neighborhood for days!

If feeding individual plants in the spring, a concentrated organic fertilizer, such as a blood, fish, and bone mixture, does the job nicely. And if any plant needs a top-up feed in the summer, add some foliar feed—liquid fertilizer applied as a spray to foliage—to each watering can of water.

UNDERSTANDING FERTILIZER NUTRIENTS	
Most over-the-counter plant foods contain some nitrogen, some potash, some phosphates, and a small amount of trace elements. The exact ratio of each is printed on the packet and this will help you to decide what to buy.	
Nitrogen	Leafy plants need nitrogen to stay lush and green. The more the plant is grown for its foliage, the higher the percentage of nitrogen required. Bamboos, palms, and any large-leafed plants such as fatsias and bananas need lots of nitrogen.
Potash	This helps plants to flower and fruit. Plants that would benefit from a high percentage of potash include cannas, agapanthus, and hedychiums.
Phosphates	This helps the root system to grow and is most beneficial to trees and shrubs. Phosphates are best applied in the form of bonemeal sprinkled into the bottom of the planting hole prior to planting.

Watering

There is no easy rule that tells you how much and how often to water plants. You cannot simply say, "two watering cans at 3pm every Wednesday afternoon." Several factors must be taken into consideration.

Growth During the months when a plant is actively growing, it will need to be watered quite regularly. When a plant is dormant, usually during the fall and winter, its water requirement is very low.

Weather Everyone knows that watering is a necessity in hot weather. But even during the winter, if it hasn't rained for a few weeks, then newly planted trees and bamboos will need to be watered.

Soil type The amount of water that can be held in the soil depends on its structure. Soil can be made up of particles of varying sizes. Small particles such as clay are capable of holding large amounts of moisture, which can easily cause waterlogged conditions. Larger particles such as chalk hold on to far less moisture resulting in soil that dries out very quickly. It is important to check which soil type you have and, if necessary, improve the structure. (See pages 14–15, Preparing the Soil and Mulching.)

An automatic irrigation system makes watering plants less of a chore.

> **TIP**
>
> Apart from not watering at all, the next worst thing you can do is to water often using very small quantities. This method of watering results in most of the water evaporating off and failing to reach the roots. Most plants, especially newly planted trees, shrubs, and bamboos, need a good drenching followed by a few days of nothing.

Pot plants Plants grown in terracotta pots, and other such containers, require far more watering than those planted in the ground, which are able to draw upon water reserves in the soil.

Drought-resistant plants With such plants, their drought-resistant quality applies only after the plant has become established. For the first couple of seasons, however, they will still need watering during dry weather.

If a plant has any special watering requirements, these will be indicated in the plant directory. However, getting to know each of your plants and their particular needs, through observation and experience, is a gardener's best source of information, so try to find out your plant's likes and dislikes.

Automatic irrigation

Apart from the obvious watering cans and hosepipes, automatic irrigation systems are now widely available and reasonably priced. For gardeners who are too busy to water regularly or spend long periods of time away from home, these systems are virtually essential. Garden centers usually stock such things if you would prefer to assemble one yourself, or a specialist irrigation company can visit your garden, advise on the best system, and install it for you. These automatic irrigation systems can be pre-programmed to come on for as long as you wish and at any time of the day or night, in the same way that a hot water timer works in the house.

If you are planning to automatically irrigate a few isolated containers, then go for a drip system that has individual inserts for each pot. If, on the other hand, you are looking for a system for the whole garden, then leaky pipes are better. These are laid all around the garden, then buried under mulch to hide them from view. The pipes are perforated so that water oozes in all directions, watering every plant within reach. Whichever system is right for your garden, you will no longer have to burden kindly neighbors with watering duties if you happen to be away on vacation!

Support

Trees

Most newly planted trees require some sort of support against the wind until the roots have taken hold. The correct way to plant and support a tree is described in the planting section on pages 14–15.

Climbers

The other group of plants most likely to need support are climbers. There are two main types of climbing architectural plants: self-clinging climbers and those that require trellis or wire support.

Self-clinging climbers produce aerial roots along the stems to hang onto rough surfaces like brickwork. These include *Pileostegia viburnoides* and *Hydrangea seemannii*. There is no need to tie in this type of climber, just direct them toward the surface you want them to climb and let them get on with it. Plants should come with a cane, then all you do is plant them at an angle, leaning toward the wall or fence, still attached to the cane.

Climbers that wind themselves around trellis or wires attached to a fence include *Clematis armandii* and *Holboellia latifolia*. These type of climbers must be tied in

> **TIP**
>
> Be adventurous with your choice of support for your climbing plants. As well as trellis, climbers can be trained up through different-colored netting, an intricate wire arrangement, a free-standing pyramid in wood or raffia, a tripod of natural wood canes, and, of course, a variety of brick or stone walls and wooden fences.

when first planted and will usually require tidying up as they grow. New shoots naturally grow in one direction, upward to the sun. To spread the plant out evenly and neatly, these new shoots will regularly need to be tied in and manually wound around the trellis or wires. As new shoots follow the sun, wind them in a clockwise direction or in a few days they will have unwound themselves.

Weeding

Each gardener has a slightly different idea of what constitutes a weed. Some may consider speedwell, buttercups, and scarlet pimpernel to be weeds, while others look on them as welcome wildflowers. Perhaps it's fair to describe a weed as simply a plant growing where it is not wanted. Weeds need to be removed, however, as they may be ugly and untidy, but more importantly they try to poach water and nutrients from other plants. The following tips will help make the job as painless as possible:

- Mulching around plants can help prevent weed seeds growing—bark chippings are especially good for this, but the mulch layer must be at least 3in (7cm) thick
- Weed regularly—do not leave it for months until the weeds are overgrown and sapping the vitality of your plants. Little and often will make it much less of a chore
- Hoeing is good for getting rid of annual weeds, but not so effective for perennials, and there is greater risk of disturbing plant roots
- Weeding by hand, with the help of a fork, is more efficient for getting rid of perennial weed roots and minimizes the disturbance to the plant.

Pruning

Pruning is usually carried out either to keep the plant neat and tidy or to control its size (see also Brown-bitting, pages 22–23). Pruning is rarely done hard enough or frequently enough. Most of us are too worried about causing harm to our plants. In fact, killing a plant through too much pruning is surprisingly difficult. If trees and shrubs have been left to get leggy and thin, cutting back a mere ⅜in (1cm) will make no difference whatsoever. Hard, serious pruning is the only way to help plants regain their bushiness.

Pruning also refers to the task of removing any dead wood or branches growing in the wrong direction, or thinning out a plant if too many branches have been produced. Pruning is not only done to make a plant denser but sometimes to make it thinner, too.

This vast subject could fill many books, but a few basic points to remember are:

- Deciduous plants (plants that lose their leaves in the fall) should be pruned when they are dormant. Early spring is best, although in mild areas pruning can be carried out as soon as the plant loses its foliage in the middle of the fall. Pruning is usually done to keep the plant in a tidy, balanced shape e.g. *Ficus carica* and *Albizia julibrissin*.
- Evergreen plants need to be pruned according to when they flower—there's no point chopping all the flower buds off. Summer-flowering plants, such as *Myrtus apiculata* and *Magnolia grandiflora*, should be tidied up in late spring before the buds form. Early-flowering

Small-leafed trees and shrubs can be cut back with shears.

Large-leafed trees and shrubs should be pruned with pruners.

plants, such as *Acacia dealbata* and *Daphne odora* 'Aureomarginata', should be pruned as soon as they finish flowering in early spring. Plants that flower in the early summer, such as *Pittosporum tobira*, could be clipped in mid-spring or after flowering in late summer.
- Plants grown for their foliage only, such as eucalyptus, could be pruned any time during the growing season.
- Herbaceous (nonwoody) plants, such as *Canna indica*, should be cut right back to the ground after the first frosts have scorched their leaves.
- Container plants, such as *Corokia* x *virgata* and *Baccharis patagonica*, can be clipped into a controlled bushy shape to make them more suitable for growing in containers. These should be clipped little and often throughout the growing season.

Winter Protection

The best advice to ensure that your plants survive the winter is to follow the hardiness guides in the directory section and choose plants appropriate for the climate you live in. If all the plants you select have to be cut back or covered up over the winter, this rather defeats the object of growing architectural plants in the first place, which are supposed to give year-round interest. That said, you may find one or two plants are just too irresistible to live without. To ensure their survival, wrapping them up for the winter is the best solution.

When to wrap?

There is no hard-and-fast rule when to wrap up a plant for the fall or winter—it all depends upon the local climate and the hardiness of the plant. First, find out the average minimum temperature for your area during the fall and winter months, and compare this with the hardiness ratings of vulnerable plants. If a plant is hardy to 23°F (-5°C), one frosty night of 21°F will not kill it, but if a prolonged spell is forecast, then it will need to be wrapped. So the best advice is: pay attention to the weather forecast!

The "work of art" method: *Musa basjoo*

Protecting your plants through the winter need not mean looking at piles of old pallets and bubble wrap for several months of the year. The following method of wrapping will create a feature of this practical necessity with something approaching "installation art" in your own garden!

In this example, the plant wrapped artistically is a hardy Japanese banana (*Musa basjoo*), one of the most exotic plants you can grow. As this plant is root-hardy, however, it is not strictly necessary to wrap it up. Simply cutting it down to the ground will ensure its survival, and it will grow back each year to a fair height.

C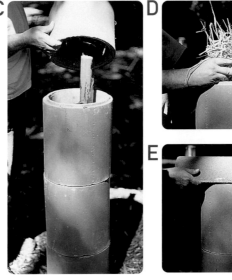

D

E

To gain the spectacular sight of the plant in full fruit and flower, however, you must retain and protect several years' growth.

The time to wrap is usually sometime during late fall, when the leaves have been slightly damaged by the first hard frosts of the year.

You will need to obtain flue liners from your local plumber (about five per plant), a ridge tile from a hardware store, and a bale of straw.

1. Remove all the leaves, cutting back close to the stem, so that just the trunk of the banana tree remains [A].
2. Position the first flue liner around the stem [B] and stuff straw into the cavity between liner and stem. Build up with more flue liners and straw [C] until the top of the stem is reached [D].
3. Finish off at the top with the ridge tile [E]. This is to prevent rain from seeping into the tower and rotting the main trunk.

And for a truly finished work of art, a group of three or four plants growing in the same part of the garden, all wrapped up for the winter!

A

B

The inexpensive method:
Cordyline australis

The method of winter protection described for bananas is ideal for small gardens where every plant is on display throughout the year. For larger gardens where many plants are hidden from direct view, a less expensive method can be used, which is particularly useful if you are wrapping large numbers of plants.

The cabbage palm (*Cordyline australis*) is another increasingly common addition to exotic gardens. However, in a really serious freeze, these could be in trouble. If planted directly into the soil, they nearly always re-shoot, but they can take many years to return to former glory. If very cold weather is forecast, usually in deepest mid-winter, treat as follows:

You will need a ball of string and a roll of agricultural fleece—available from most garden centers—and a stepladder may also be required for taller plants.

1. Scoop up the foliage [A] and tie it with string to keep it together [B]. This ensures that all the younger growth inside is fully protected from cold weather.

A

2. Wrap several layers of agricultural fleece around the plant [C]. Secure it with string and cut off the fleece from the roll.

3. Tie the fleece in several places to prevent winter gales from blowing it away [D].

B

D

C

Protecting tree ferns

The other most common subjects that gardeners wish to grow in areas often far too cold for them are tree ferns, such as *Dicksonia antarctica*. Outside of urban centers in warm areas and mild coastal regions, they cannot be expected to survive unprotected during an average winter in a temperate climate.

Tree ferns grown in pots can simply be moved somewhere frost-free for the winter, such as a conservatory, greenhouse, or utility room. For specimens growing in the ground, two methods of protection can be considered:

1 **Either:** wait until the fronds have frosted and gone brown, then cut them off as near to the trunk as possible. The most vulnerable part of the plant is then at the tip of the trunk, just inside the hollow bit at the top, where the new fronds will emerge. To keep this area frost-free, gently push straw or burlap into the hollow, and fasten with string (see picture above).

2 **Or:** you will need to obtain a decent number of straw bales. Pull up the fronds vertically and secure them with string. Then stack the bales as tightly as possible around the trunk, gradually building them up to conceal both trunk and fronds. The finished article will look like a miniature haystack.

TIP

Straw is great insulation and heat can start to build up inside very quickly, so as soon as temperatures rise, make sure you remove the straw straight away. Otherwise the heat could start to cook the foliage, leaving a soggy mess that will have to be cut off and putting an end to all your hard winter protection work.

Brown-Bitting

There is little information around on the subject of how to improve the looks of architectural plants. Yet "brown-bitting" a plant—"manicuring" the foliage by, literally, removing all the brown bits—will turn a well-grown, healthy specimen into an even more stunning addition to the garden. As such, brown-bitting should be regarded as an integral part of general care for architectural plants.

Most keen gardeners understand the principle of removing untidy branches from trees or cutting off old, dead growth from herbaceous perennials, but a certain timidity sets in when it comes to cordylines or yuccas. Old and scruffy foliage is often left on the plants, not out of laziness, but due to a lack of understanding of what can be achieved, or perhaps for fear of harming them in some way. But with a few tweaks here and a snip or two there, the difference can be astonishing.

Basic technique

Cordyline australis is a prime candidate for brown-bitting. If the older leaves are not removed, they turn brown, droop down, and start to build up on themselves to form a bushy thatch. The best time of year to carry out the brown-bitting is late spring or early summer, when

the plants are growing, as any accidental damage done will heal over more easily.

Starting with the older lower leaves first, take a very sharp knife or some pruners, pull the leaf taut and cut as near to the stem as possible [A]. Remove the leaves one at a time gradually moving up the trunk [B]. When every brown leaf has been trimmed away [C], remove any old flower stems, too.

If the plant has never had its old leaves taken off in this manner, the whole process can take several hours, but the final appearance will be well worth the effort.

Sculpting

By following the technique described above, an untidy, shrubby cordyline can be transformed into a very exotic-looking tree with several beautiful corky tree trunks, previously hidden from view. Yet the potential for brown-bitting need not end there. The technique may also be employed creatively to give a sculpted appearance to a plant.

For example, yuccas have lovely fleshy leaves that are white inside. The yucca, in the example shown below, is a very shabby looking plant [A]. If great care is taken to trim all the leaves using pruners to within

just an inch (3cm) of the trunk [B], an attractive "pineapple" effect finish can be formed [C]. When only green leaves are left, the result is often a very exotic shape, with gnarled woody bark as a stem.

Tree ferns often have highly sculptural trunk "bark." *Dicksonia antarctica*, for instance, has a very wide trunk with a lovely fibrous, dark chocolate-colored bark, while *Dicksonia squarrosa* has a delicate, slender trunk with an almost black bark. By cutting back all the old, brown fronds of a tree fern hard to the base, the plant will look so much more lush and cared for, and the great beauty of the trunk will be revealed in all its glory.

The most important lessons to be learned in sculpting a plant is to go gently at it and banish your fears of harming your plant. In most instances you will simply enhance both its looks and its health.

Trimming palm leaves

Palms can receive the brown-bitting treatment in two ways. Firstly, by cutting off the old dangling yellow and brown foliage right back to the base as previously discussed. Secondly, each individual leaf can be manicured, which sounds an incredibly time-consuming project, but one that is definitely worthwhile when the end results are seen.

Fan palms such as *Trachycarpus fortunei* and *Chamaerops humilis* often have brown tips that form at the ends of leaves, particularly if the plants are grown in a pot. Lightly trimming the ends of each leaf with a pair of scissors can extend the smart appearance of a palm fan by several months (*below*).

Manicuring palm leaves.

When you come to attempt this job, make sure that your scissors, or preferably pruners, are as sharp as possible. The cut on each leaf of a fan should be as straight and as level as you can make it. If your chosen implement is slightly blunt, you could end up tearing the leaves and make them appear even shabbier than with the brown bits on them!

If you trim the fans of your palm regularly, leaves may start to look too small after two or three trimmings. At this stage the entire fan should be chopped off, right back to the base of the leaf stalk. Be ruthless and rest assured that you are not harming your treasured plant—removing the brown parts of a leaf is encouraging your architectural palm to become an even healthier and stronger plant. And not only that, you are improving its appearance, making your palm look even more striking in your garden, patio, or conservatory.

23

Propagation

Many amateur gardeners enjoy growing their own plants. It is not usually done for financial reasons, but for the feeling of pride and sense of achievement having raised plants with your own hands. Although some types of propagation, such as micropropagation or the raising of ferns by spores, is out of reach for most gardeners, other methods can be done with only a modicum of experience. Propagation is one of those horticultural skills that has an air of mystery surrounding it. In fact, common sense and strict hygiene practices are all that are often required for many of the plants featured in this book.

only reason for failure would be if you thought it might need a drop more water—but this nearly always has fatal results.

To test if the offset has rooted, give it a tug and if there is any resistance, then roots must have formed. Once it has fully rooted, repot it in a small pot filled with a soil-based potting mix and a handful of extra grit added for drainage [D]. You can now start watering it in the usual way. Make sure you treat the baby plant gently, as new roots are very easily damaged.

Other species of agaves and yuccas can also be propagated from offsets using the same method.

TIP

Taking offsets from succulents such as agaves should be performed regularly for container plants. With the parent plant sending out "babies" from its base, the pot will become quite crowded and the root system coiled and compressed. The main plant may also need to be repotted into a slightly bigger container after taking offsets.

From offsets: *Agave americana*

Offsets are the baby plants sent up from underneath the soil from the base of the plant. They are part of the parent plant and will therefore be identical to it.

Agave americana frequently produces offsets from its base. In mid-spring, take the plant out of its pot [A], select a healthy-looking offset at least 2in (5cm) long, trace it back toward the parent plant, and remove it with a very sharp and very clean knife as near to the main plant as you can reach [B]. Try not to hack at it, but cut it off cleanly with a single cut. The cut end will be moist. Lay out the offset on a sunny windowsill for a few days until the cut end has dried out. This will lessen the chance of any rotting taking place. Then push the base into a pot of gritty soil [C], mixed from equal quantities of general purpose potting soil and fine gravel. This sharply drained mix should eliminate any danger of the offset rotting away. Water in gently and then do absolutely nothing until it has taken root, which should take a couple of months. The

By division: *Arundo donax*

Propagating by division is the separation of a single plant clump into several sections, each one of which will produce a new plant.

The example shown here involves digging up a well-established, mature clump of *Arundo donax* (*right*) from the garden in early spring using a garden fork and dividing it into new sections. Spring is always a good time to do this, as the plant is just at the beginning of its growing season, which will ensure that each new division gets off to a quick start.

Make sure you dig down far enough beneath the plant to lift under the roots [A]. Take care when you are doing this as the plant is likely to be quite weighty. Try and keep the roots intact at this stage. Next, place the clump of roots down on a nearby path or an area of ground in the garden with nothing planted in it. Using a sharp saw or an ax, chop the plant into even sections, with each section comprising one or two canes [B].

Plant up the individual chunks, each with their own smaller root system [C], into pots of loamy soil or straight back into the garden if new planting sites have already been chosen. Plant these sections at the previous depth of the main plant before they were taken out of the ground.

Cut the canes hard back, removing all foliage except at the growing tip, and plant each individual section so that each cane can just be seen poking out of the ground [D]. This will ensure that all of the plant's energy

Arundo donax

goes into producing new growth, instead of having to sustain all of the old canes and foliage. Keep the plants moist, and new growth should start again in late spring or early summer.

Don't try this method on bamboos, which are a different prospect altogether. However, other tough grasses, such as the pampas grass (*Cortaderia selloana*), can easily be split in this manner.

TIP

This type of division is successful for most clump-forming plants and grasses. Take care when separating this type of plant not to damage the fine roots. Cut the rhizomes (the rootstock) into pieces that all have at least one shoot and dust the cut surfaces with powdered fungicide. Pot up with the rhizome below the surface and shoots exposed.

From seed: *Canna indica*

Growing plants from seed can be a gamble, not just with regard to success but also because of the variable results that can be produced. They will not be exact replicas of the plant from which the seedhead has been removed. This could lead to disappointment in some cases, but since you can't be sure of the results you have the excitement of possibly producing new forms. This is often the case with named varieties, which tend not to "come true" from seed, although it also happens less frequently with the straight forms of plants. Some plants, such as eucalyptus, can only be produced by this method because cuttings are always unsuccessful.

Fresh seed is essential. Some types of plants can be produced from seed that is many years old, but fresh seed usually guarantees a higher success rate. Either gather your own seed from a *Canna indica* in the garden

TIP

Many plants can be propagated by seed. Some of the easiest to practice with are *Echium pininiana*, *Acanthus mollis*, *Euphorbia mellifera*, and *Phormium tenax*. Follow the same steps as given below. Soaking seeds can help speed up germination but it is important that once soaked, they should be sown immediately.

or buy from a reputable seed company. Mature plants will produce seed pods shortly after flowering. When these have ripened, collect and store them in the fridge until early spring. To check that they are ripe, open up a pod and look at the contents. The seeds should be dark brown, hard, and shiny. Sowing is best done in late winter or early spring.

Soak the seeds in warm water for 24 hours. This will break down the hard outer seed case and hasten the germination process. Pot up singly into small 3½in (9cm) pots, scrubbed clean and filled with sterilized seed starting mix, or else use a seed tray with firmed down starting mix [A]. Sprinkle the seeds on to the mix [B]. Push each seed down with a finger until it is about ⅜in (1cm) under the mix [C]. Sprinkle more starting mix over the top until it is completely hidden [D]. Water lightly. Place the tray or pots into a small propagating unit [E], which can be obtained cheaply from most garden centers, and set the temperature to 70°F (20°C). The warmth will help to speed up the production of new seedlings, which takes much longer in cooler temperatures.

Seedlings should be large enough to handle by the end of spring and can then be repotted into larger pots and put outside or planted directly into the garden. They should flower the same year. In colder climates, wait until the danger of frost has passed before planting them outside.

Ripe seed pods of *Canna indica*.

From cuttings: *Phillyrea latifolia*

Propagating from cuttings will produce a plant that takes on the same form as its parent. It is a useful method in many ways, particularly for trees that can otherwise take years to produce fresh seed. The advised time for taking cuttings is very important to pay attention to, as some plants will only root at certain times of the year, depending upon the maturity of new growth. Some deciduous plants, such as the common fig, will only root from cuttings taken when the plant is in a dormant state after the leaves have been shed for the winter.

When new growth of *Phillyrea latifolia* has ripened, usually in early fall, remove the tips of each shoot with very sharp, clean pruners. Each tip should be about 3in (7.5cm) long. Take several cuttings, not just one, as results are rarely successful every time. Remove leaves from the lower half [A] and trim the bottom of the cutting, diagonally across and up, to just under what was the lowest leaf joint. (The picture to the right shows how the cutting should look once the lower leaves are removed and the new stem has been cut straight under the lowest leaf joint.) Dip the bottom ⅓in (1cm) into some hormone rooting powder, which can be bought at all good garden centers [B].

Fill a 3½in (9cm) pot with seed starting mix and firm down to form a flattened surface. Push the cuttings in so that the mix reaches to just under the lowest remaining leaves [C]. A pot this size will take five cuttings around the outer edge and one in the middle. Water in gently and place the pot in a cold frame for

the winter. They should start to root the following spring and can be potted up individually later the same year.

Other plants that are worth trying by this method are *Magnolia grandiflora*, *Laurus nobilis angustifolia*, and *Myrtus apiculata*. For evergreen, broad-leafed plants and conifers, semi-ripe cuttings are best taken in late summer or fall from stems that have thickened and become harder. Take them from the parent plant just above a node. They should still be soft at the top but firmer at the base. Follow the steps as illustrated here for *P. latifolia*, removing the lower sideshoots from the stem, and transplant into individual pots before placing in a propagator or cold frame.

View of a *Phillyrea latifolia* cutting.

> **TIP**
> All cuttings should be inspected regularly, with the pots or container trays watered if the seed starting mix or cutting mix shows signs of drying out, for example shrinking away from the edges of the container. If the cuttings are in a cold frame, this may need added insulation over the winter, such as a burlap cover.

Planting Combinations

Some gardeners design their gardens along a particular theme that reflects their enjoyment of a certain type of plant. For example, lovers of spiky or succulent plants not only collect these plants, but also enjoy creating gardens in which they appear more natural. By mulching around the planting scheme with fine grit or gravel rather than leaving the soil bare, for instance, the impression of an arid or desert climate is created in which the plants look more "at home." Similarly, jungle plants look especially good in gardens where the lawns have been dispensed with in favor of pathways made from thick layers of chipped bark.

Many gardens, however, are simply made up of a mix of all types of plants according to the gardener's whim. There is absolutely nothing wrong with this. So long as the gardener is blissfully content with the final result, that is really all that matters. Gardens are very personal creations, and rules and regulations have no place there.

The only piece of advice I consider essential is to read and learn as much as possible about the type of plants you intend to grow—to make sure that they are suitable for the amount of sun, shade, space, and shelter that can be offered. The rest is pure common sense. For example, it goes without saying that planting a tiny plant that grows to no more than 3ft (1m) behind one that will eventually reach 10ft (3m) is not very sensible!

A mixture of tall, lush, and spiky plants can be used to achieve a jungly, rainforest effect.

The exotic, tropical-looking flower of *Magnolia grandiflora*.

Jungle combinations

For damp, slightly shady gardens with rich, fertile soil, aiming to create a jungle look with architectural plants is easily achievable. This type of setting is normally crammed full with plants in every possible space: free-standing, climbing into and clambering over each other, and trailing along the ground. It is a style of garden that can look very effective, but care should be taken so that enough room is left for people to walk through. The plants also need to be ruthlessly managed as they mature, with adequate pruning and brown-bitting carried out. A lush, green mass with plenty of height from trees should be aimed for, together with plants that provide movement and rustling sounds such as bamboo. Why not think about the scents that can be found in a jungle garden, too, a good example being the deliciously fragrant flowers of *Magnolia grandiflora*?

Desert combinations

For sun-baked gardens with free-draining soil, desert-type plants are ideal. The Sonoran Desert in southwest USA is one of the most beautiful settings in the world, and the desire in some gardeners to mimic this type of landscape is entirely understandable. Each plant has plenty of light and space around it. The plants have all adapted in some way to cope with the low rainfall, often by producing large fleshy leaves in which water can be stored. These sparsely distributed plants have also learned how to protect themselves from local wildlife by developing barbs and sharply pointed tips on their leaves.

Desert plants have some of the most strongly architectural shapes of all plants, and plenty of room should be left around them in order for their dramatic outlines to be appreciated to the full. Have a look at the table for some inspiring ideas.

Spiky, drought-resistant plants create an instant impression of the desert.

Mediterranean combinations

For sunny, well-drained gardens to evoke the south of France and Tuscany. A typical Mediterranean garden would be planted to give shade during the summer months when temperatures soar. Scented plants are often a feature of this kind of garden. Height is provided by the umbrella pines and Italian cypress, which are not only beautiful to look at but also have aromatic foliage. Scent is also provided by magnolias, pittosporums, and climbing plants such as trachelospoermum. Loud, vibrantly colored flowers are usually commonplace, too. The color and fragrance found in a Mediterranean garden can produce a very sensual effect.

Sculpted aromatic plants help define a Mediterranean feel.

Seaside combinations

Gardening on the coast presents a real challenge, as any seaside dweller will know. Strong winter gales coming straight off the ocean will quickly shred any large leaves, while the salty air can make many plants look scorched and brown. However, with a bit of careful planning, a seaside garden can be made to look interesting year-round, and can easily be emulated by city gardeners who wish to be reminded of vacations spent at the shore.

Full sun and sharp drainage are essential in a coastal garden, and planting should generally be quite sparse. Plants with lots of dense foliage are needed, under-planted with tough, salt-resistant ground cover, plus the occasional large and leathery-leafed spiky plant for a bit of drama. Many of the most suitable choices come originally from New Zealand, where they have survived the salty coastal breezes for centuries. Gray- or blue-leafed plants also feature heavily in the list of suggestions (see bottom of the opposite page). The best way of complementing the final planting is to mulch heavily with large pebbles of the size and color found on a typical beach.

Scented combinations

Everyone loves fragrance in the garden. A walk through a garden that greets you with different perfumes is a sensual experience. It should not be too difficult to plan the planting so that there is something scented in flower year-round, even in the depths of winter, when the promise of a delicate fragrance is the only thing likely to tempt many gardeners outside on a freezing cold day. Aromatic leaves are also important in scented gardens. A stroll around the garden after breakfast can be very pleasurable if there are plenty of leaves within reach that can be crushed or rubbed to release their pleasantly pungent odors.

Japanese combinations

Japanese-style gardens are becoming increasingly popular. They are quiet, calm places that offer the chance to meditate and reflect on life for a few peaceful moments. The soothing sound of water is often present. A comfortable place to sit, tucked away in a hidden corner, is also desirable. Instead of a lawn, the ground is covered with small stones that can be slowly raked into a neat pattern. Just a few carefully chosen specimens are planted, which should always be meticulously cared for. Fallen leaves, brown bits, or untidiness of any kind is not permitted!

CHOICES FOR JAPANESE COMBINATIONS

Aralia elata, Clematis armandii, Cyperus alternifolius

Fatsia japonica, Holboellia coriacea

Mahonia lomariifolia, Ophiopogon planiscapus 'Nigrescens'

Phillyrea latifolia, Phyllostachys aurea, Phyllostachys nigra, Pittosporum tobira, Podocarpus salignus, Pseudosasa japonica

Sasa palmata nebulosa, Trochodendron aralioides

CHOICES FOR SCENTED COMBINATIONS

For aromatic leaves choose:

Cupressus sempervirens 'Pyramidalis', *Eucalyptus aggregata, Eucalyptus niphophila* 'Debeuzevillei'

Ficus carica, Laurus nobilis angustifolia, Lyonothamnus floribundus asplenifolius

Melianthus major, Myrtus apiculata, Rosmarinus repens

For fragrant flowers choose:

Acacia dealbata, Acacia pravissima, Albizia julibrissin, Azara microphylla, Baccharis patagonica

Clematis armandii, Colletia cruciata, Cordyline australis, Cynara cardunculus

Daphne odora 'Aureomarginata', *Eriobotrya japonica, Euphorbia mellifera, Genista aetnensis*

Hedychium coccineum 'Tara', *Holboellia coriacea, Holboellia latifolia*

Magnolia grandiflora, Myrtus apiculata

Pittosporum tobira, Trachelospermum jasminoides

The delicate, scented flowers of *Trachelospermum jasminoides.*

Bamboos & Grasses

Bamboos and grasses have an essential role in exotic gardens. Apart from contributing their visual leafy presence, many of them add movement and noise. Listening to the sound of the breeze rustling through a large clump of bamboo is always a pleasurable experience.

All bamboos are evergreen, providing a permanent architectural presence in the garden and offering a variety of other uses. They make excellent screening plants, not only to give privacy, but also to reduce noise from passing traffic. They look good planted as single specimens in smaller gardens, especially those that have colored canes, or planted in large groups near ponds and lakes. They are also a wonderful choice for children's play areas, especially if planted in avenues. They can be pulled about and charged through, without the plants or the children coming to any harm.

Bamboos have a reputation for being very invasive. Although this is true of some of them, many are well-behaved clump-forming species that can be used quite safely in suburban gardens. They do, however, all have one thing in common—their insatiable demand for copious amounts of water. Without this, they will quickly turn brown and die (just think of what happens to a lawn during a dry summer).

Grasses have much gentler demands and mostly just sit there looking beautiful. They vary enormously, from the tiny leaves of the black grass to the aristocratic-looking Pampas grass. All are suitable for a wide range of planting schemes.

✳ Arundinaria anceps

(syn. Yushania anceps)
Anceps Bamboo

Lovely cascades of soft, evergreen foliage make this bamboo very desirable. It can be grown either as a single specimen or massed together for screening. The leaves are so plentiful that it can even be trimmed to form a thick hedge. This extremely hardy plant is fast growing and can fill a large space very quickly. Maximum height is usually no more than 12–15ft (4–5m).

Select a good-sized specimen for planting, as small seedlings are often difficult to get going. Choose a sheltered site out of strong winds. The more sheltered the planting position, the greener and healthier the foliage will look. Do not allow this bamboo to dry out, especially during the first couple of seasons. Feeding is also important, and every four weeks

soil	Growing this plant in fertile, manure-enriched clay soil gives excellent results
site	Sun or light shade, and ideally in a sheltered position out of the wind
watering	It is crucial that this plant is never allowed to dry out
general care	To prevent it growing too high or spreading too far, clip with shears to keep under control
pests & diseases	Check regularly throughout the growing season for green aphids. Spray at the first sign

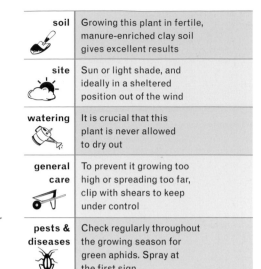

Arundinaria anceps

from mid-spring to early summer a few handfuls of a blood, fish, and bone mix should be sprinkled around the base of each plant. If grown as a hedge, clip regularly throughout the growing season.

Flowering rarely occurs, which is a good thing because plants usually die after flowering. Bamboos are often re-classified and given an even sillier name than before. With this in mind, always buy bamboos from reputable nurseries to ensure that they have been labeled correctly with the name that is presently in favor.

Arundinaria anceps

❋ Arundo donax

Giant Reed

A huge grass that can grow to 13ft (4m) tall and has thick canes a good 2.5cm (1in) in diameter. It looks a bit like sugar cane with its blue-green foliage and leaves nearly 2ft (60cm) long. The plant's energy goes into producing height rather than width, and it is quite slow to form a decent-sized clump.

A. donax is very hardy and is especially useful for coastal areas. It can withstand sea winds extremely well and during strong breezes, the leaves whip around against the canes making a wonderful noise. During the winter, the leaves turn brown and two choices can be made: either strip the foliage from the stems leaving just the bare canes, or cut the whole lot down to ground level. It will start to regrow in mid-spring and quickly reach its full height again in one season.

Watering is necessary for the first couple of seasons after planting, but the plant is then capable of looking after itself so that feeding and watering can largely be ignored. *A. donax* will grow almost anywhere. It is often seen growing in water-filled ditches and along riverbanks in warmer climates. It can even grow in sun-baked clay.

soil	Prefers soil that is rich, moist, and fertile, but is tolerant of most conditions
site	Sun or shade, but particularly good for exposed positions
watering	Although not too fussy, does appreciate lots of moisture
general care	Remove any brown leaves as they appear. Can be fed in mid-spring with a mixture of blood, fish, and bone
pests & diseases	Relatively trouble-free. Pests and diseases do not usually cause any problems

Arundo donax

A variegated form is often available with pale cream stripes across the leaves. This is less hardy than the green form and reaches only 7ft (2m) in height. Dried *A. donax* reeds are occasionally used for the ceilings in barns and houses in some European countries.

Arundo donax

❋ *very hardy*

✳ Cortaderia selloana

Pampas Grass

Although some gardeners shun Pampas grass, considering it an inferior plant in rather poor taste, this seems unfairly dismissive of a truly wonderful grass. It can form massive clumps that make an imposing addition to any garden. Enormous quantities of long, arching, evergreen leaves quickly pile up on themselves to form a graceful architectural shape. Leaves are sharply edged and glaucous green. Clumps can reach 10ft (3m) across. This is a very easy plant to grow.

In early fall, tall panicles start to emerge from the center of mature plants. These can reach 10ft (3m) tall and open up into large, fluffy plumes of a rich cream color. They can be cut and dried for indoor flower arrangements.

C. selloana is very forgiving of most planting sites, provided that it is sheltered from strong winds. However, these plants will perform much better if they are grown in rich, moist loam with adequate irrigation. Older clumps can become untidy and should be given a savage haircut every other year in early spring. Cut the whole clump down to ground level with powerful electric hedge-cutters. If this becomes too difficult to do, you could burn the clump down. This will quickly deal with all the

Cortaderia selloana

	soil	Largely unfussy but performs best in fertile, rich loam
	site	Likes a sheltered and sunny position, protected from strong winds
	watering	Regular irrigation should be carried out until the plant has fully established
	general care	Feed with general balanced fertilizer once a year in mid-spring. Cut off dead plumes after flowering has finished
	pests & diseases	Relatively trouble-free. Pests and diseases do not usually cause any problems

Cortaderia selloana

brown thatch that gradually accumulates from old leaves. New foliage soon grows up again.

There are various dwarf or colored forms often available, but none manage to match the splendor of the true Pampas grass. This plant is still sometimes listed as *Cortaderia argentea*.

✳ *very hardy*

35

Cyperus alternifolius
Umbrella Plant

A pretty little perennial grass like a miniature Papyrus, only much tougher. It is surprisingly hardy for a plant whose native country is Madagascar. *C. alternifolius* can be grown outside throughout the year in mild city gardens and most coastal areas. This plant forms clumps of long, bright green stalks that can reach 3ft (1m) tall. These are topped with spreading "umbrellas" of grass, so that the whole plant looks like a group of tiny palm trees. Flowers are typical grassy tufts and are not particularly exciting.

If grown outside, either grow it in a pond or a very boggy site where it has permanent access to water. It will die down each year and send up new shoots in spring. This plant can also be grown

soil	Unfussy. Can be grown in a boggy area, near a pond, or indoors in a conservatory
site	Is suitable for full sun or light shade in a sheltered spot
watering	Must never be allowed to dry out—impossible to overwater
general care	A very easy plant to care for. Chop off old leaves at the base when they become untidy
pests & diseases	Fairly trouble-free, but look out for aphids on the new growth during spring and early summer

very successfully indoors in the conservatory, where it remains evergreen. Stand it in a large saucer of water and never allow it to dry out. This plant is particularly suitable for gardeners who kill their plants through kindness, because it is impossible to overwater.

Although there are the usual methods of propagation—such as using division or else by fresh seed—there is another way that is much more fun to try, especially for children. Chop off one of the heads from the plant with a long piece of stalk attached. Turn it upside down and push it into a bottle filled with water. Roots will form from what was previously the top, and new shoots will start to grow from the center. Always keep the water fresh and clean so that the whole process can be observed. When a manageable-sized plant has developed, take it out of the bottle and pot it up in fresh potting mix.

Word of warning: it is common practice in many nurseries that grow plants of this kind in containers to add a chemical called Suscon Green to the potting mix. This is to kill certain pests that can be a real problem to plants grown in pots. Unfortunately, this chemical is also dangerous to fish and other aquatic life.

Cyperus alternifolius

❄ *tender*

❄ Ophiopogon planiscapus 'Nigrescens'

This is a plant that would please even the most design-conscious gardener. The leaves really are jet black. They form little tufts of coal-colored clumps that slowly spread to cover areas of no more than 3ft (1m) with a maximum height of only 6in (15cm). Groups of this lovely grass look particularly effective in beds mulched with colored grit or stones.

The almost unpronounceable *O. planiscapus* 'Nigrescens' is evergreen, and apart from the unusual colored foliage this grass has attractive sprigs of lilac flowers in late summer, which are followed by small, shiny, black berries that last for months.

To get the very best from these slow-growing plants, put them in a sunny position in fairly light soil. As with all plants, they perform much better when planted directly into the ground, but these grasses could also live quite happily in a pot for many years. This unfussy plant is virtually maintenance-free.

It can be tempting for many gardeners to try and obtain as many different plants as possible, thereby creating what is sometimes seen as an interesting and varied collection. This is fine for botanic gardens, but to create a good display in an average garden, it is much better to plant larger numbers of fewer species. Plants such as *Ophiopogon planiscapus* 'Nigrescens' are very desirable, but because of their tiny size, they could easily be overlooked if just one or two are planted. A large drift of them, however, would have much more impact and make a noticeable and stunning display.

Ophiopogon planiscapus 'Nigrescens'

Ophiopogon planiscapus 'Nigrescens'

soil	Light, sandy, and well-drained, preferably in the ground, but can tolerate pots	
site	Full sun preferred in a sheltered position but tolerates partial shade	
watering	This type of grass is fairly drought-tolerant once established	
general care	Feed with a small amount of general fertilizer in mid-spring but is generally quite easy to care for	
pests & diseases	Usually trouble-free. However, it is worthwhile checking for aphids during the summer	

❄ Phyllostachys aurea

Golden Bamboo

As well as being a good-looking bamboo, *P. aurea* is also an extremely versatile plant. It has thick canes with attractive knobbly bits on them (correctly called clustered node bases) and masses of delicate-looking foliage. It has a very vertical habit and stays in tight clumps at the base, making it suitable for even the smallest of gardens. It is a wonderful plant for screening purposes and can quickly hide ugly fence panels or provide privacy from neighbors. Because it is non-invasive, it could just about qualify as a suitable candidate for a pot, provided that the container is enormous and has automatic irrigation.

Despite its common name, the canes usually remain green, except in very hot climates, when they can take on a golden hue. Maximum height is unlikely to be more than 16ft (5m). If grown as a screen, plant at a distance of one plant per 5ft (1.5m). Frequent irrigation is essential, although

Phyllostachys aurea

once fully established, watering will normally only be necessary if there is a prolonged drought. Feed with a mix of blood, fish, and bone or any high-nitrogen food every four weeks from mid-spring until early summer. Avoid planting in a windy position to ensure that the foliage remains green and healthy.

Bamboo canes emerge from ground level at the thickness they will always be—the girth does not increase as it ages. With this in mind, it is a good idea to cut out all thin or weak-looking canes, leaving only the sturdy fat ones. This can be done at any time of the year.

Phyllostachys aurea

soil	Growing this plant in fertile, manure-enriched clay soil gives excellent results
site	Full sun or light shade and in a position sheltered from the wind
watering	Never allow to dry out, especially during the first few seasons after planting
general care	Remove older brown leaves as they appear. Once established, this is normally an easy plant to care for
pests & diseases	Aphids are frequent visitors. Check new growth regularly and spray at the first sign

❄ *very hardy*

❋ Phyllostachys aureosulcata 'Aureocaulis'

This is arguably one of the most attractive bamboos, especially for a small garden. New canes are tinged a lovely pinkish-red color, which gradually ripen to a deep butter yellow. Canes are produced at an extraordinarily prolific rate, easily sending up around eighty in only five years. As with many *Phyllostachys* bamboos, the clumps stay nice and tight at the base, so that even the smallest town garden could accommodate one of these remarkable plants.

The leaves are tiny and massed in such quantity that they can be clipped to form a hedge. Single specimens look rather interesting if trimmed lightly up the sides with the crown shaped into a rounded dome, like a giant jellyfish. However, as the height is likely to reach only 16ft (5m), they can also be left to grow naturally and enjoyed as they are. Shelter from strong winds always improves the appearance of any bamboo, although this one is more tolerant of breezy conditions than most.

New plants should be watered thoroughly throughout the year—they do not like to dry out at all, even during the winter months. After a few years, however, irrigation will normally only be necessary during the growing season. The application of a high nitrogen food from mid-spring to early summer will give very pleasing results. Propagation is not that easy for the amateur gardener, but dividing the plant up into sections in early spring might occasionally be successful. At the beginning of each season as new shoots are emerging, a lot of foliage forms around the base. Trim this off as much as possible so that all the canes remain clearly visible. They are, after all, the plant's best feature.

Phyllostachys aureosulcata 'Aureocaulis'

Phyllostachys aureosulcata 'Aureocaulis'

soil	Prefers soil that is rich, fertile, and moisture-retentive
site	Full sun produces the best colored canes. Protect from very strong winds
watering	Must never be allowed to dry out, especially before becoming well established
general care	Remove any rhizomes that appear outside the main clump to maintain a neat and tidy appearance
pests & diseases	Check the growing tips regularly for aphids during the spring and summer. Spray at the first sign

❋ *very hardy*

Phyllostachys nigra

Black Bamboo

Although the foliage of *P. nigra* is perfectly acceptable, it is the canes that make this particular bamboo so popular. Mature clumps have numerous straight, thick, black canes, which many gardeners find irresistible. After a shower of rain, they become darker and glossier and even more beautiful. This is a slow plant to get going, but once the roots are fully established, growth accelerates rapidly. Individual specimens can reach 16ft (5m) in height and have a spread of 4ft (1m) after 6–8 years provided that their cultivation requirements have been met.

This very hardy bamboo prefers a sunny spot in rich, moist, fertile soil in a sheltered position completely out of the wind and out of the way of people brushing past it. If planted in an exposed site, the small leaves quickly become desiccated and brown around the edges, giving it a scruffy and uncared-for appearance. Ample supplies of water are essential throughout its life to get the very best from this plant. Several handfuls of a blood, fish, and bone mix sprinkled around the base every four weeks from mid-spring until early summer are also beneficial. Strip any lower leaves away from the canes up to a

soil	Growing this plant in fertile, manure-enriched clay soil gives excellent results
site	Full sun or light shade and in a position sheltered from the wind
watering	Permanent access to water is essential—never allow to dry out
general care	Remove older brown leaves as they appear. Once established, this is normally an easy plant to care for
pests & diseases	Aphids are often a problem in spring and summer. Check new growth regularly and spray at the first sign

Phyllostachys nigra

height of about 3 or 4ft (1m) to make the color of the canes even more visible. Cut out any thin or weak-looking canes as soon as they appear. This ensures that all the goodness from the food and water is distributed only to the superior ones. New canes are quite green at first and gradually ripen to their ebony color after their full height is reached. To speed up the blackening process, canes can be chopped off at 8ft (2.5m). This does no harm at all—it just produces a shorter, more manageable plant, which may be even more suitable for a small garden.

Other varieties such as *P. nigra* 'Henonis' and *P. nigra* 'Boryana' are often available. Lovely though they are, be warned: their canes are nowhere near as black as those of the true *P. nigra*.

Phyllostachys nigra

very hardy

❄ Pseudosasa japonica

Tall and imposing bamboo that can quickly reach 14ft (4m), and one of the most forgiving bamboos available, hugely tolerant of the sort of conditions that bamboos usually dislike. Leaves are long and strap-like and, although the slender canes are green, these are almost totally concealed by numerous pale brown papery sheaths. The stems have a graceful arching habit that provide a wide spreading canopy of at least 10ft (3m) across the top of each clump. *P. japonica* is fast growing and is perfect for screening purposes. Although it can spread across wide distances, it is easy to keep confined to a small area. As soon as a shoot appears where it isn't wanted, it can simply be snapped off at ground level. If mature plants become too dense, any unwanted canes can be thinned out by cutting them off at ground level with pruners. This can be done at any time of the year.

Copious amounts of water are preferred but this bamboo is quite happy if irrigation is overlooked from time to time. Windy, exposed conditions can be tolerated without too much damage to the leaves. In fact, fierce gales bring the added bonus of experiencing the loud rustling noise made as the wind swishes through the entire plant. Any planting site can be chosen, from full sun to deep shade, and most types of

Pseudosasa japonica

soil will suffice. However, very poor, chalky ground will need frequent applications of manure to ensure good results.

Pseudosasa japonica

soil 🔧	Largely unfussy but poor, chalky soil will need the addition of manure
site ⛅	Happy in full sun or shade, not bad for exposed coastal gardens
watering 💧	Prefers lots of water, but can cope with occasional neglect
general care 🛒	Appreciates an annual feed with well-rotted manure or anything with a high nitrogen content
pests & diseases 🐞	Aphids adore it—growing tips and undersides of leaves should be checked during spring and summer

❄ *very hardy*

❊ Sasa palmata nebulosa

A tropical-looking bamboo with enormous leaves that look as if they could never survive a cold winter. However, this plant is hardy virtually anywhere. Although the foliage is tempting, be warned: this is one of the most thuggish and invasive bamboos available and the planting site should be chosen with great care. Once established, it is difficult to eradicate. The maximum height of the canes is about 8–9ft (3m) and each leaf could be up to 1ft (30cm) long and 3in (7cm) across, which is the largest leaf of any hardy bamboo.

S. palmata nebulosa can spread rapidly and is totally unsuitable for small gardens unless confined to a massive pot. If grown this way, divide and replant clumps regularly, and every few years chop the whole plant down and let it start again. Automatic irrigation and lots of high nitrogen food will also be necessary to keep the foliage bright green and glossy.

Sasa palmata nebulosa

If grown in the ground, make sure it has ample space to spread itself around. If it becomes necessary to remove it, try cutting it down to ground level and dig a large trench all around its perimeter. Fill this trench with something salty, such as fresh seaweed. Hopefully, this will start to kill it off fairly quickly, although a couple of attempts may be needed. This bamboo is so tough that even after flowering it just carries on as normal, unlike other bamboos which usually die.

Sasa palmata nebulosa

soil	Any soil type will do, but rich moist soil preferred if grown in a pot	
site	Will grow anywhere but light shade is best in a sheltered position	
watering	Does not like to dry out—imperative to keep plant well irrigated	
general care	Remove any brown leaves as they appear. Feed annually with manure or a blood, fish, and bone mix	
pests & diseases	Relatively trouble-free. Pests and diseases do not usually cause any problems	

❊ *very hardy*

Ferns
& Palms

Ferns and palms are obvious choices for exotic gardens. Nothing conjures up a tropical image more than a palm tree. The idea of being able to plant one outside in a cold wintry climate has almost universal appeal. They add an immediate vacation feel to the landscape and can be planted singly in small town gardens, in groups around outdoor swimming pools, or in larger groves in suburban or country gardens.

Small, seedling palm trees are not for impatient gardeners because they are all very slow-growing. Decent-sized plants of at least 3ft (1m) should always be acquired if the budget allows, not only for instant effect, but also because they are much hardier than tiny specimens. Ferns are happiest in quiet, shady, damp corners where most flowering plants refuse to grow. They like peat, and although for environmental reasons this is best avoided, sometimes nothing else will do. All the ferns described here are evergreen, so their delicate fronds can be appreciated throughout the entire year. They all need adequate supplies of water, although none of them will tolerate permanently boggy sites.

Ferns and palms have one essential requirement in common—they hate being in the wind. Palm fronds get battered and torn and look messy. Ferns fronds just shrivel and turn brown. With the notable exception of the Dwarf Fan Palm (*Chamaerops humilis*), all should be kept well away from the sea front.

❄ Blechnum chilense

An absolute monster of a fern, which could reach a height and spread of more than 3–4ft (1m), provided that it is given the right conditions. The surface of the fronds is rough to the touch and puckered like seersucker fabric. Ferns can be fussy plants and *B. chilense* is certainly no exception. Shade is essential to keep the fronds a good color. Although low temperatures can be coped with, milder climates are preferred, together with a super-abundance of available water. Waterlogging, however, will not be tolerated at all, so good drainage is very important with this fern. It is tricky to get the watering exactly right—too much will lead to rotting and blackened leaves, too little and the plant will shrivel. Planting on a bank or slope in a high rainfall area and out of the wind would be a perfect choice.

The soil should be very light and crumbly, but using just peat is not a very good idea, as this type of soil dries out too quickly and is often difficult to re-wet. An ideal mix would be equal quantities of leaf mold, peat, and loam. Leaf mold is a bit of a luxury and not always easy to acquire, but the search is well worth the effort. All ferns are happiest planted directly into the ground, but if this is not possible, use a very

soil	Light and crumbly—an ideal mix would be equal parts of leaf mold, peat, and loam
site	A shady position, sheltered from wind but where air circulation is good
watering	Plenty of moisture, but with perfect drainage so excess water runs away immediately
general care	Does not usually require feeding, and any older brown fronds should be removed as plants age
pests & diseases	Relatively trouble-free. Pests and diseases do not usually cause any problems

large pot and do not firm the soil more than necessary. Fern roots are extremely lazy things and prefer their journey through the soil to be made as easy as possible. Humidity is appreciated, but try to avoid getting the fronds too wet in very cold weather, as this can cause the leaves to blacken. Feeding is not usually required. Propagation is extremely difficult, particularly for the amateur, as freshly ripened spores are needed for the process.

Blechnum chilense

❄ *hardy*

✳ Blechnum spicant

The Hard
or Deer Fern

A fully hardy evergreen fern with bright emerald green fronds fashioned in the shape of a fish skeleton. The maximum height is unlikely to be more than 18in (45cm), and individual clumps can spread slowly to just 2–3ft (60cm) across. The new growth in the spring is particularly attractive. New fronds uncurl to reveal an even more startling bright green than the adult foliage. As these plants are usually planted in the shade, this vivid coloring brightens up the whole area, which is an especially refreshing sight after a

soil	Neutral to acid soil that is light in texture. Chalk or lime will give poor results
site	This fern is happiest in the shade but can tolerate some sun
watering	Needs moist but not boggy conditions, can cope with drier conditions
general care	Does not usually require feeding, and any older brown fronds should be removed as plants age
pests & diseases	Relatively trouble-free. Pests and diseases do not usually cause any problems

gloomy winter. *B. spicant* is a frequent sight in woodlands. This fern is happiest in the shade and grown in moist, peaty soil with leaf mold added if available. Shade and moisture is preferred, but this tough little fern can cope with drier conditions and will even tolerate some sunshine. Neutral to acid soil is necessary—chalk or lime in the soil will give very poor results. If the local water supply is from an area with a high pH, then avoid using tap water. It is worth buying a water butt to collect rainwater. Provided that this is kept scrupulously clean, ferns can be watered with the contents of this instead, which should keep them happy.

Try to choose a sloping site for this plant, so that all excess water can drain away immediately. Apart from that requirement, this is an exceptionally easy fern to grow. No annual feeding is necessary, and pests and diseases are not usually a problem.

These plants are commonly found in woodland, but should never be removed from their natural habitat. Instead, always purchase them from a reliable and reputable nursery. Propagating ferns is always difficult without professional expertise but if this is available, make sure that fresh spores are used. These usually ripen around early fall. Plant these ferns in large groups.

Blechnum spicant

✳ *very hardy*

❄ Brahea armata

Blue Hesper Palm

A very beautiful desert palm whose leaves really are blue—a lovely silvery blue, making *B. armata* a very desirable acquisition. It is very slow-growing and tends to survive rather than thrive in temperate conditions. Low temperatures down to 14°F can easily be tolerated, but the rain, fog, and general murk of many winter climates makes the choice of site very difficult. Being a desert palm, it is more used to crisp dry air—a different sort of cold altogether. If grown in a mild climate, plant near to a wall or a house to shield it from the worst of any wet weather. Otherwise, it is best grown in a large pot and overwintered indoors or under glass.

Full sunshine and very gritty, well-drained soil is essential. Because of its slow speed of growth, very little annual maintenance is required except for a couple of handfuls of blood, fish, and bone sprinkled around the base in mid-spring. If planted directly into the ground, it becomes extremely drought-resistant once established. If it is to spend all its life in a pot, however, this drought resistance never develops, and regular watering throughout the summer is essential. Keep fairly dry from the middle of fall to early spring. In the wild, *B. armata* can reach up to 12m (40ft) but the height in general cultivation is unlikely to exceed more than 3m (10ft).

Brahea armata

When purchasing one of these lovely palms, choose a decent-sized specimen. Great patience will be required to wait for a small one to grow as it can take 15 years to reach 2m (6ft). Some nurseries list this under its old name of *Erythea armata* or sometimes *Brahea glauca*.

Brahea armata

soil	Free-draining, gritty soil is essential for this palm to grow well
site	Full sun out of strong winds or indoors in a sunny conservatory
watering	If grown in a pot, water regularly during the spring and summer seasons
general care	Use a balanced fertilizer once a year in mid-spring. Remove any older fronds that have turned brown
pests & diseases	Keep a lookout for red spider mite as these can become a nuisance if the plant is grown under glass

❄ *tender*

✳ Butia capitata

The Jelly Palm

A fine, stately palm with blue-gray arching leaves. It is surprisingly hardy for such a glamorous-looking tree and should do well down to 14°F, provided that it is kept fairly dry during the winter, which is often difficult in many climates. This is why it has been given a "category red" code to warn gardeners to be cautious. If grown in a cold area, it would be better to keep it in a large pot and overwinter indoors or under glass. When the plant and pot become too heavy to move, planting directly into the ground is the only option. In severe winters, the whole plant can be tied up and shrouded in agricultural fleece until spring returns.

Full sun is essential, with the added back-up of heat reflected from a warm wall if possible. Very well-drained soil is another essential requirement, although watering must be done liberally for the first couple of seasons until it settles in. Very little maintenance is required except for the removal of any old and untidy leaves and an

soil	Free-draining loam is essential for this palm whether indoors or outside
site	A sheltered position in full sun outdoors or in a bright conservatory
watering	Once established, fairly drought-resistant outdoors. Water regularly if in a pot
general care	If grown outside, winter wrapping is necessary. Feed annually with a mix of blood, fish, and bone
pests & diseases	If grown under glass, be on the lookout for red spider mite and scale insects

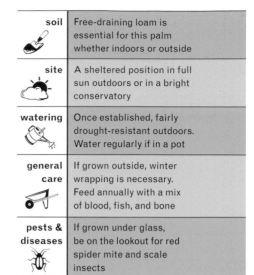

Butia capitata

Butia capitata

annual application of food sprinkled around the base of the trunk in mid-spring. Away from its native habitats of Brazil and Argentina, the overall height is unlikely to reach more than 13ft (4m).

As *B. capitata* is so slow-growing, try and save up to buy a decent-sized specimen. Nurseries sometimes list this as *Cocos corinata*, *C. australis*, or *C. capitata*.

✳ *tender*

Chamaerops humilis

Dwarf Fan Palm

A low-growing bushy palm that sends up numerous suckers around the base throughout its life, rather than forming a single trunk. This palm is a familiar sight along the French and Italian Riviera where it can easily reach 13ft (4m). In colder climates, a more realistic expectation of height at maturity is only around 6–8ft (2m). Foliage is plentiful and the whole clump can become very dense, enabling it to withstand strong winds, making it a brilliantly suitable palm for coastal districts. The color of the foliage is very variable, ranging from green, silvery-green to almost blue. Sometimes these plants have such generous dustings of silver over the fronds, it looks as if someone has sprayed them with metallic paint. During warm summers, after flowering, clusters of large, orange, shiny berries are produced.

C. humilis prefers full sun, although the fronds stay a prettier green if grown in light shade. Small plants can struggle to get through a cold winter, but larger specimens are much hardier. As this palm is so slow-growing, it is a reasonably good choice for growing in a pot on a balcony or terrace. On older plants, buried inside the thick clumps of leaves, trunks start to develop very slowly. As these are rather attractive, plants can be pruned to remove some of the surrounding offsets to expose these hairy offerings. Generous amounts of high nitrogen food are essential in spring and early summer.

Young palms are often confused with *Trachycarpus fortunei* and are sometimes wrongly labeled at nurseries and garden centers. Check the petioles (leaf stalks) before buying—*C. humilis* will have vicious thorns all the way along.

Chamaerops humilis

Chamaerops humilis

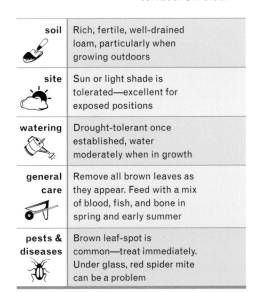

soil	Rich, fertile, well-drained loam, particularly when growing outdoors
site	Sun or light shade is tolerated—excellent for exposed positions
watering	Drought-tolerant once established, water moderately when in growth
general care	Remove all brown leaves as they appear. Feed with a mix of blood, fish, and bone in spring and early summer
pests & diseases	Brown leaf-spot is common—treat immediately. Under glass, red spider mite can be a problem

❄ *hardy*

❄ Dicksonia antarctica

Tasmanian Tree Fern

This amazing fern is one of the world's most beautiful plants. A thick, fibrous, chocolate-brown trunk is topped with huge, deeply cut fronds 7ft (2m) long. *Dicksonia antarctica* starts to form a trunk after five years. This grows at a rate of only 1ft (30cm) every ten years, so buying a baby plant will need a lot of time and patience to see it develop into something spectacular.

This fern is extremely fussy in its requirements—it is almost like buying a pet. Shade is essential, so is a sheltered position, not only out of the wind but also away from anyone brushing past it. Humidity is very important and ideally the trunk should be sprayed twice daily during the hot summer months. Mild gardens are necessary to keep it outside year-round. Otherwise, keep it in a very large pot and overwinter in a shady, cool conservatory. Alternatively, follow the winter wrapping method using straw bales as described on pages 20–21. Water to keep the soil just moist. The occasional application of a balanced dilute liquid feed poured into the top of the trunk can have a remarkable effect on how many new fronds are produced— twice the normal number can be expected.

The fronds should remain evergreen for several years, but if the ideal cultivation conditions cannot be met, fronds are quite likely to go brown. If this happens, cut them

Dicksonia antarctica

off at their base and try to treat next year's new fronds with a little more care.

Because many thousands of *D. antarctica* are taken from forest clearance sites in Tasmania and Australia, buying from a reputable nursery hopefully assures the customer that these are not being sold illegally. If there is any doubt at all as to their origin, leave them where they are and buy from somewhere else.

Dicksonia antarctica

soil		Peat mixed with leaf mold and silver sand to help with the drainage would be ideal
site		Shade and shelter from wind. Avoid planting where people can brush against it
watering		Regular irrigation throughout the growing season, particularly in hot weather
general care		Apply liquid feed every month from spring until mid-summer. Wrap up in winter (see pages 20–21 for more details)
pests & diseases		Relatively trouble-free. Pests and diseases do not usually cause any problems

❄ *tender*

Phoenix canariensis

Canary Island
Date Palm

An imposing palm whose appearance most people find appealing and a vital addition for mild city gardens or warm coastal areas. Huge, arching fronds burst out of a giant "pineapple" base and older trees eventually form a trunk, although this takes many years to achieve a decent height. Small plants are not at all hardy, but once the overall size reaches 6–7ft (2m) much colder weather can be tolerated. In warmer climates, date-like fruits are produced, but these are inedible.

Full sun is essential and the soil must be exceptionally well drained. Waterlogged conditions would be an automatic death sentence. Salty sea gales do not seem to be much of a problem. As this palm is unsuitable for a pot for more than a couple

soil	Fertile, well-drained loam is preferred, particularly for growing outdoors
site	Full sun is best for this palm. Good for exposed windy positions
watering	This palm is remarkably drought-resistant once it has become established
general care	Remove any older brown fronds. Feed in mid-spring with a few handfuls of blood, fish, and bone around the base
pests & diseases	Relatively trouble-free if grown outside. Red spider mite and scale insects could cause problems if grown indoors

Phoenix canariensis

Phoenix canariensis

of years, planting directly into the ground is a must. In colder areas, winter-wrapping is the only answer. All the fronds are pulled up vertically and tied into place, so giving the more delicate inner leaves protection from frost. Further details and instruction can be found on pages 20–21. Propagation is only possible from seed.

Although the removal of any older brown fronds sounds a simple enough task, the reality can be an awkward process. The leaf stalks can become very woody and the base can be several inches across. As the leaves should be cut right back to their base, a saw is the only option.

 tender

❄ Trachycarpus fortunei

Chusan Palm

A magnificent palm that is totally hardy once it reaches around 3–4ft (1m). The solid, hairy trunk is topped with enormous fan-shaped leaves, making it an essential addition to any exotic garden. Permanent access to water is required, whether by automatic irrigation or by growing along the bank of a stream or near a pond. A sunny spot encourages faster growth, but a shady site does no harm at all. Lower light levels make the petioles (leaf stalks) become elongated, giving a more jungly appearance.

T. fortunei is a greedy plant and almost impossible to overfeed. Treat it to large dollops of rotted manure or several handfuls of blood, fish, and bone every four weeks during spring and early summer each year. This will speed up the growth, which is usually very slow. Maximum height for most colder climates would be around 25ft (8m) but this could easily take thirty years. Not suitable for growing in containers for more than a few years.

Mature plants start to flower annually in late winter. These take until late spring to fully form and resemble giant yellow smoked haddocks hanging out of the center of the growing point. These look most bizarre and

Trachycarpus fortunei

can either be left to enjoy or removed, so that all the plant's energy goes back into the leaf-making process, which is put on hold until after flowering. This palm is very easy to grow, but it does have one requirement: it must be protected from wind. The leaves are so enormous and fragile that constant battering by winds makes the whole thing look very messy and untidy. Its idea of hell would be to live on a sea front.

Many outlets now stock this plant and it is sometimes labeled with its old name of *Chamaerops excelsa*. Its common name refers to the area of China where it was first discovered.

Trachycarpus fortunei

soil	This palm grows best in soil that is rich, fertile, moist, and loamy
site	Prefers sun or shade away from strong or cold, drying winds
watering	Needs to have constant access to water. Does not like to dry out
general care	Remove any old brown leaves from the plants and feed well from early spring to early summer
pests & diseases	Relatively trouble-free. Pests and diseases do not usually cause any problems

❄ *very hardy*

Climbers

All of these climbers have been chosen for their exotic-looking foliage. Some have large jungly leaves, some have smaller delicate-looking leaves that mass together to provide a dense covering. Many of these plants also have exquisitely perfumed flowers. If *Clematis armandii*, Holboellias and Trachelospermum are all planted together, heavily fragranced flowers will waft perfume around the garden from late winter until the middle of fall almost without a break.

Climbing plants are invaluable for hiding hideous fence panels, sheds, drainpipes, and other unsightly objects. All of the climbers here are evergreen so their cover is permanent. Some are self-clinging, others will need the assistance of a few wires or trellis to help them on their way. Not only are they useful, but they are also beautiful additions for the garden, adding a bit of much needed height to many smaller town gardens.

As they are usually pinned flat against walls or other surfaces, none of them takes up very much space in the garden. Therefore, not only is there room for several different varieties, plenty of space is left for lots of other plants, too, whether they are trees, palms, or herbaceous specimens. They associate just as well with either spiky agaves or lush bamboos and make subtle additions to any style of garden.

Provided that their individual watering requirements are met, all are easy to care for.

Clematis armandii

A very vigorous, large-leafed, evergreen climber that can grow just about anywhere. It is not self-clinging, but can quickly wind itself around drainpipes and trellis or up through trees, easily reaching a height of 15–20ft (6m). The flowers are borne throughout spring, and can even appear as early as late winter if the weather has been mild. They are pure white, very lightly fragrant, and up to 2in (5cm) across.

Although virtually any soil will suffice, this is one of those rare plants that actually seems to prefer to grow in chalky or alkaline conditions. Sun or shade are both acceptable, but more flowers will be produced in a sunny spot. There seems to be a lot of complicated pruning instructions for many clematis: not so for this one. Simply chop it back when it outgrows the space allocated for its height and spread. *C. armandii* produces its flowers on growth made the previous year, so do any pruning after the flowers have finished in late spring. As older plants tend to get a bit woody around the base, it is a good idea to occasionally wind a few new shoots downward to provide a constant replenishment of foliage to keep it from looking too bare. Never let this plant dry out. Watering should be done regularly during its first couple of seasons. Thereafter, the roots should find their own supply.

Clematis armandii

There is a popular variety called *C. armandii* 'Apple Blossom', which has pale pink flowers. Pretty it may be, but it is very prone to virus, causing the leaves to curl and look unsightly. The straight pure white form is much more vigorous and robust, and therefore more reliable.

soil	Well-drained alkaline soil is preferred, but this plant will grow in virtually any soil
site	Sun or shade in a sheltered position—the more sun, the more flowers
watering	Regular watering is required for the first couple of seasons until established
general care	Give a light sprinkling of blood, fish, and bone mix or equivalent around the base annually in late spring
pests & diseases	None as a rule, but check for whitefly if buying a plant that has been grown under glass

Clematis armandii

❄ *very hardy*

C

Climbers

❄ x Fatshedera lizei

A large-leafed, evergreen jungly climber that can either climb up trellis or be left to scramble across the ground, where it can quickly trample over every weed or cover every scrap of ground in its path. It is a cross between *Hedera helix* 'Hibernica', which provides its robust qualities, and *Fatsia japonica* 'Moseri', from which it inherits its good looks. (Crossing two species means it is a bi-generic hybrid, to give it the correct horticultural terminology!)

This plant adores shady conditions in a sheltered spot and the lower the light levels, the richer emerald green the leaves become. Odd-looking cream-colored flower spikes are produced in the fall but, as these are not things of great beauty, they can be removed so that all the energy goes into leaf production instead. Rich soil is preferred and copious amounts of water will be required especially for the first couple of years until the roots settle in.

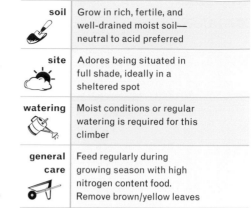

soil	Grow in rich, fertile, and well-drained moist soil—neutral to acid preferred
site	Adores being situated in full shade, ideally in a sheltered spot
watering	Moist conditions or regular watering is required for this climber
general care	Feed regularly during growing season with high nitrogen content food. Remove brown/yellow leaves
pests & diseases	Black aphids can be a problem on the new shoots of this plant in early summer

Although fully hardy, a late frost can burn the new growth. If this happens, chop off any damage—don't worry, it will soon send up more new shoots.

Black aphids are such regular visitors to this plant that it is best to assume that they will definitely appear at some time. With this in mind, check the new shoots almost daily throughout the end of spring. At the very first sign of aphids, cut off the end of the growing tip where they congregate. New shoots will soon be produced again, normally within a couple of weeks. Chemicals should only be used as a last resort if large plagues of insects have built up due to lack of regular inspection.

x Fatshedera lizei

❄ *very hardy*

❄ Holboellia coriacea

A vigorous, hardy, evergreen climber from China that belongs to the family with one of the most fantastic names in horticulture—Lardizabalaceae. It grows almost anywhere, the dark green leathery leaves look good in a sunny or shady situation. Growth is dense and can provide thick cover quickly, so that walls or fences are totally blotted out. Wires or trellis are needed for the wiry stems to wind around as they are not self-clinging, and just one plant can easily travel several feet.

Impatient gardeners, however, should plant one every 6–7ft (2m) if there is a large area to conceal. Flowers are dangly bunches of pretty purplish-white that have a chocolate fragrance on still, sunny days. These can appear as early as the beginning of spring and last for many weeks. During early fall, after a hot summer, odd swellings sometimes appear on mature plants. These start off as green, knobbly "walnuts" and expand into long purple "potatoes," which look quite bizarre. They are edible but as they taste rather bland, they are best left on the plant to impress the neighbors.

Although happy in acid or alkaline conditions, better results are achieved on plants grown in rich, fertile soil. An annual dressing of well-rotted manure applied in the spring is very beneficial. Newly planted climbers take a while to settle in and all the energy goes into the roots for the first season. However, the following year demonstrates admirably why it is classed as fast-growing. Frequent watering is essential for the first year but after then, it largely takes care of itself and watering should only be necessary during hot, dry summers.

Holboellia coriacea

Holboellia coriacea

soil	Tolerates any soil, but happiest in rich, moist, and fertile conditions
site	Sun or shade but must be kept sheltered from very strong winds
watering	Frequent watering during its first year. Drought-resistant once established
general care	Generous amounts of rich food in spring. Prune only if the plant outgrows its allocated space
pests & diseases	Aphids can be a problem on new shoots but generally trouble-free from other pests and mites

❄ *very hardy*

❋ Holboellia latifolia

A wonderful evergreen climber blessed with many virtues. Foliage is a very dense mass of fresh green, slightly leathery leaves that lay flat to the wall or fence. Growth is remarkably vigorous, once the roots have settled in, and can easily cover an average sized fence panel in three years. Stems can twine around wires or trellis quite easily if given a bit of coaxing in the right direction to start with. Individual shoots can reach 20ft (6m), so covering drainpipes or growing up trees is no challenge at all to this energetic plant. Mature lower stems eventually form into a gnarled woody trunk.

The fragrance from its flowers is so strong that an entire garden can be filled with exquisite scent, similar to Gardenia, with just one plant. Flowers are either pale greenish-white if male, and tinged pink if female—both smell delicious. They last about 6–8 weeks during spring. On mature plants or after a very warm summer, peculiar-looking fruits appear during early fall. They start off pale green, the same color as the leaves, so they are not immediately obvious. These knobbly "potatoes" gradually enlarge until they are 4–5in (10cm) long, then they ripen into a bright pinkish-purple color in the middle of fall. Although edible, they taste rather unexciting so are best left on the plant to enjoy visually.

Pruning can be done at any time of year. No rules of technique are needed—just chop bits off it when it is in the way or becomes untidy.

Holboellia latifolia

Holboellia latifolia

soil		This plant tolerates any soil but prefers well-drained soil that is rich, moist, and fertile
site		Sun or shade, can cope with quite windy sites reasonably well
watering		This climber is fairly drought-resistant once it has become properly established
general care		Appreciates very generous amounts of well-rotted manure applied annually in spring
pests & diseases		Aphids can be a problem on new shoots but generally trouble-free from other pests and mites

H. latifolia is sometimes confused with other Holboellias and also Stauntonias to which it is related. In fact, it was previously named as *Stauntonia latifolia* before being correctly categorized. When offered for sale, it usually has the support of a bamboo cane in its pot. Leave this on—after a couple of seasons it will soon be concealed.

❋ *hardy*

✳ Hydrangea seemannii

Large-leafed evergreen climber that is self-supporting, clinging onto walls by aerial roots that form all along the stems. Although recently introduced from Mexico, this plant is fairly hardy, easily surviving occasional blasts of 14°F. The big, glossy leaves can completely smother a wall or even the entire front of a house, but this will take many years. *H. seemannii* is an unbelievably slow starter. Newly introduced plants do virtually nothing that is visible for the first full season. Instead, all the initial energy goes into establishing the roots. For the next three or four years, growth will still be slow, and could spread as little as 5ft (1.5m) in all directions. Thankfully, it then speeds up a bit so that after ten years it could easily be touching the gutters on the first floor.

The conditions also have a marked effect on this plant's performance, which will be faster on rich, moist soil than on drier,

soil		Will grow in any soil but prefers rich, fertile, and moist conditions
site		Unfussy—all sites tolerated but stays a much better color in full shade
watering		Needs adequate moisture for at least the first three years after planting
general care		Feed with well-rotted manure each spring. Tie into position when first planted, until it starts to self-cling
pests & diseases		Leaf spot can be a problem and affected leaves should be removed at the first sign

Hydrangea seemannii

chalky ones. As this climber is usually planted right next to a wall, where it is often quite dry, watering should be thorough for at least the first two or three years. This is an ideal plant for a shady spot, where it is more likely to send out aerial roots at a younger age. Sunny walls are fine, but the plant will need a bit of coaxing in the right direction before it gets a grip. Flowers are splendid frothy creations that are usually produced in the summer. They are pale cream and a mass of tiny flowers clustered together. They are similar to the blooms produced by the delicate Lace-cap varieties of Hydrangea, rather than the loud, brightly colored ones that appear on the types frequently found growing in coastal gardens. As they can take rather a lot of energy away from the leaves, hardhearted gardeners can remove them as they appear—if they so wish. *Hydrangea seemannii* is easily propagated from semi-ripe cuttings.

Hydrangea seemannii

✳ *hardy*

✳ Muehlenbeckia complexa

M

Climbers

An exceptionally versatile plant that will adapt to many different sites as well as being useful for quickly obliterating unsightly features. The tiny evergreen leaves form a very tight mass obscuring everything behind or beneath them. Ugly fences, half-derelict walls and dry, stony soil can soon become a distant memory. It is just as happy growing along the ground as it is twining upward on wires or through trees. It is even possible to use this plant for topiary, by wrapping it around metal frames. Its very thin wiry stems make it easy to clip into shape. Its peculiar name is all thanks to Dr Muehlenbeck, a Swiss physician, in whose honor it was named.

It is hardy in most climates except for severe frost pockets and is one of the toughest plants around for coastal areas. Strong, salty gales are just shrugged off and, in its native country of New Zealand, it can actually be found growing on the beach. It can be grown in colder areas, but does not remain evergreen during very bad winters. Flowers are white waxy bells, but are so incredibly tiny that they are difficult to spot without close inspection. A single plant growing upward could reach a height of 16ft (5m) with a 6–8ft (2m) spread.

M. complexa really does grow anywhere, as long as it is planted directly into the

Muehlenbeckia complexa

ground. It is hopeless in a pot, unless the container is enormous. It can cope with bright sun or deep shade, is happy in clay or chalky soil, will grow in moist conditions, or scramble over a dry beach. It is excellent ground cover and will romp around any other plants. Feeding is usually unnecessary.

Muehlenbeckia complexa

soil	Unfussy—can tolerate any soil type, including clay or chalky soil
site	Versatile plant that enjoys full sun as well as deep shade
watering	Water regularly during first season. After that, watering can largely be ignored
general care	No feeding or pruning necessary. It is one of the easiest plants to cultivate
pests & diseases	Keep a careful watch for aphids during a hot summer. They are fond of tapping into the new growth

✳ *hardy*

❄ Pileostegia viburnoides

This plant is a rather classy evergreen climber whose name is a good test for Latin pronunciation. It is sometimes still listed under its old name of *Schizophragma viburnoides* which does not help matters at all. This is a plant that really should be more widely grown. The large, elongated leaves are beautifully shaped with each leaf being a dark, glossy green. Foliage is plentiful, giving a thick covering for a wall or fence. Masses of cream frothy flowers appear in late summer. It makes a good choice of climbing plant for gardeners who cannot be bothered with wires or trellis because it is self-clinging and hangs on tenaciously once it is established. *Pileostegia viburnoides* grows very slowly for the first few years, but once it gets

soil		Will grow in any soil, but rich loam that is slightly acid is best
site		The deeper the shade for this climber, the better the color of the foliage
watering		Water well for the first couple of years until established
general care		Feed once a year in spring using either well-rotted manure or a mix of blood, fish, and bone
pests & diseases		Relatively trouble-free. Pests and diseases do not usually cause any problems

Pileostegia viburnoides

a hold, things speed up a bit and eventually it could cover the front of an entire house with ease.

Pileostegia viburnoides is not fussy and will grow in most gardens under almost all conditions, although much better results are produced if it is planted out in rich, loamy soil and given lots of moisture. A shady aspect generally keeps the foliage a much deeper color. An annual feed with something like a mix of blood, fish, and bone is all that is needed to keep it in good condition. Pruning should only be done in the unlikely event of it becoming too big.

❄ *very hardy*

❄ Trachelospermum jasminoides

Star Jasmine

A fine evergreen climber that has deservedly become much better known during the last few years. *T. jasminoides* has attractive leathery leaves that are small and shiny. However, it is mainly grown for its fabulous scent. Clusters of sweetly smelling, star-shaped white flowers are produced in profusion from the beginning of summer until the middle of fall if the right conditions are met. Growth is slow but fairly dense so that it can completely conceal the wall or trellis behind it. After ten years it will cover an area of only about 8ft (2m) wide and 13ft (4m) tall. If a stem or leaf breaks, harmless milky sap will exude from the injured part. Slim green seedpods

Trachelospermum jasminoides 'Variegatum'

soil	Neutral to acid and well-drained. Lime-free soil is essential
site	Light shade—too much sun bleaches leaves and too much shade reduces flowers
watering	Water almost daily during its first summer. Drought-resistant once established
general care	Feed only when the foliage needs a bit of a boost, otherwise keep it hungry to encourage more flowers
pests & diseases	Aphids a problem outdoors. Under glass, red spider mite is a nuisance. Red leaves are a sign of stress

6in (15cm) long are sometimes produced in pairs after a hot summer. In warmer parts of the United States where growth is faster, it can be seen growing as a hedge or sometimes trained as a small half-standard tree. A variegated form is also available but this is only reliably hardy in warm gardens, on the coast, or in heavily populated cities, where heat from people, cars, and pollution keeps temperatures higher.

Lime-free soil is essential, so is shelter from cold winds. Copious amounts of moisture are required until established, after which it becomes very drought-tolerant. It does not generally perform well in a pot unless the container is the size of a garbage can, due to the amount of watering that would be needed. If it really must be kept in a pot, keep it by a door that is frequently used. That way, the scent from the flowers could be sampled every time it is walked past and the chance of remembering to water it would be fairly high. If allowed to dry out, all the flowers and flower buds will drop in alarmingly high numbers.

Trachelospermum jasminoides

❄ *hardy*

Trees

No matter how small the garden is, there is nearly always room for a tree. Trees are the essential third dimension in gardens that would be very flat and dull without them. They not only add height, but can also provide a shady spot to sit under in the summer. Some can be used as windbreaks if the garden is on the top of a windy hill or near the coast. They also bring wildlife into the garden, with birds always being particularly welcome visitors. Ornamental trees can be the main focal feature of a garden and can even assist in keeping the coldest of night frosts at bay by providing a canopy to protect plants growing underneath them.

Newly planted trees are usually appreciative of at least one strong stake to support them during their first couple of seasons, and adequate irrigation should be given to all trees until they become established. Many trees are classed as drought-resistant once they become mature. Drought resistance is not a magical quality that develops, it just refers to trees becoming more self-sufficient in their quest for water. Once their roots have grown down deep into the soil, they are then capable of searching for water without human assistance, although a helping hand during periods of excessive drought is always a good idea. Hopefully, this explains why plants that are sometimes referred to as "drought-resistant" such as olives should always be well watered during their entire life if left in a pot—in pots they do not have the option of burrowing down deep with their roots to find natural reserves of water.

❄ Acacia dealbata

Mimosa

A fast-growing evergreen tree suitable for small gardens, as the maximum height in most climates is unlikely to exceed 25ft (8m). Although the ferny foliage looks delicate, it thrives in coastal areas where it can frequently be blasted by salty winds. The flowers are a familiar sight at florists as they are a mass of fluffy yellow balls during spring. They are highly fragrant. In exceptionally cold winters, this tree can be cut back to the ground by frost. However, they nearly always reshoot and can quickly regain their former height.

A. dealbata loves as much sun as it can get. Shady planting sites will produce very leggy plants that are less likely to

soil	Poor, very well-drained, and slightly acid. Chalky soil to be avoided
site	Full sun, preferably with some shelter from very exposed sites
watering	Once established in the ground, this tree becomes extremely drought-resistant
general care	No feeding required. Pruning necessary only if the tree becomes too large for its position
pests & diseases	Outdoors it is usually trouble-free. Under glass, scale insects can be a problem

Acacia dealbata

flower. A perfect planting spot would be against a sunny wall in poor, slightly acid, very well-drained soil. Chalky soil should be avoided. Although occasionally windy conditions are fine, some shelter is required from completely exposed sites. Once this tree is established, it is extremely drought-resistant and virtually maintenance-free. As poor soil is preferred, annual feeding is unnecessary. If pruning is required, do this immediately after flowering in late spring or early summer as the next year's flower buds start to form again from late summer onward.

This tree is a popular choice for conservatories, as the scent from the flowers can fill the whole room. However, the speedy growth of A. dealbata makes it very unsuitable for growing in a container unless it is pruned back hard each year. Watering is also vitally important, as drought resistance never develops unless the tree is grown in the ground. Pot-grown plants should never be allowed to dry out.

If you were to consider propagating this plant, then this is most easily done from seed. However, plants raised this way can take as long as five years to flower. An A. dealbata that is grafted, rather than grown from seed, flowers much earlier.

❄ tender

✳ Acacia pravissima
Ovens Wattle

Pretty little weeping tree with foliage quite unlike the familiar types of acacia. The evergreen leaves are tiny, flattened triangles that run the length of each stem. Flower buds start to form in early fall but stay closed tight until early spring, when they open up into masses of tiny fluffy balls that are bright yellow and very fragrant.

A. pravissima is the hardiest type of acacia there is, so it can be grown in many more locations than would normally be expected. As the ultimate height is unlikely to exceed 16ft (5m), this makes it a possible contender for even the smallest garden.

This tree adores sunshine and hates the wind, so an ideal planting place would be against a sunny wall in poor, slightly acid, very well-drained soil. Annual feeding is unnecessary. The only maintenance required is to gradually remove the lower branches to make it look more like a tree rather than a large bush. A tree is a much better option for this plant in order to show off its beautiful weeping habit. Although regular watering is required for the first year after planting, it should then start to develop its resistance to drought and can largely be ignored. If allowed to dry out soon after planting, the leaves can take on a bronzed appearance and it rarely regains full health. Pot-grown plants never develop the drought resistance of those planted in the ground.

Acacia pravissima

Acacia pravissima

soil	Poor, very well-drained, and slightly acid. Loam-based potting mix if grown under glass
site	Full sunshine. Needs shelter from the wind in exposed positions
watering	Essential for newly planted trees—drought-resistant once established
general care	Remove lower branches gradually as the plant develops, to shape it into a tree rather than a bush
pests & diseases	Relatively trouble-free. Pests and diseases do not usually cause any problems

❋ Albizia julibrissin
Silk Tree

This beautiful deciduous tree would be a stunning addition to any small garden. The large leaves look far too delicate for most climates but, despite its reputation for being tender, it has proved itself to be very tough indeed.

This tree comes into leaf rather late, usually around the end of spring, and it can start shedding its foliage as early as late summer. For this reason, it is best grown against a sunny wall, where its season can be extended by several weeks. A sun-baked position produces copious amounts of pale pink powder-puff flowers in mid-summer, which last for about six weeks and are delightfully fragrant. Long, green seedpods are occasionally

soil	Well-drained, poor soil that is neutral to slightly acid. Avoid chalk
site	Full sun, preferably against a warm wall to make full use of the sun
watering	Once established, this tree becomes extremely drought-resistant
general care	Virtually maintenance-free. Occasional light pruning can be done to keep the head a tidy, balanced shape
pests & diseases	Coral spot could be a problem. Mature plants should be checked for this before buying

Albizia julibrissin

produced after an especially hot summer. Apart from requiring a sunny spot, the soil needs to be fairly poor, well drained, and lime-free. Minimal maintenance is needed, apart from a little light pruning to keep the head a balanced shape. This should be done when the tree is dormant, either in the fall or just before the new growth starts in the spring.

Its ultimate height could eventually reach a maximum of only 25ft (8m), which makes it very suitable for even the smallest town garden. The variety *A. julibrissin* 'Rosea' is often available. This is more of a dwarf form, reaching a maximum height of around only 16ft (5m). It has slightly darker pink flowers.

Albizia julibrissin

❋ *very hardy*

❄ Aralia elata
Japanese Angelica Tree

Words like shapely and sculptural would aptly describe this lovely Japanese tree. The leaves are huge, over 3ft (1m) long, and beautifully crafted into delicate leaflets along the length of each stem. The plant is very hardy and, although deciduous, still makes a very worthy contribution to any exotic garden. The slim, rarely straight trunk is covered with thorns even into maturity, making it rather an odd sight especially in the winter after the leaves have dropped. Clusters of cream-colored flowers appear in great profusion during late summer.

Although often seen as a multistemmed shrub, it is far superior when grown as a single-stemmed tree. Height, even at maturity, would be a maximum of only around 20ft (6m). Rich, moist soil in light woodland shade would be ideal for *A. elata*. It is a very slow-growing tree so little annual maintenance is required, apart from the occasional feed. Keep in a sheltered position out of strong winds, which could

Aralia elata

tear the leaves. Suckers from the roots can be removed to keep the plant single-stemmed. These can be kept and used for propagation. Regular checks should be made for even the slightest damage from capsid bugs. It cannot be overemphasized how much these horrid creatures can ruin the appearance of the foliage (*see* pages 152–157 for further details).

When purchasing one of these lovely trees, try and buy one during its dormant period after the leaves have dropped. The leaves are very delicate when fully unfurled and so transporting them home in one piece is always difficult.

Aralia elata

soil	Light, manure-enriched, free-draining soil gives the best results
site	Woodland shade, preferably in a sheltered spot out of strong winds
watering	Keep soil moist for first few seasons. Fairly drought-resistant when established
general care	Feed annually in spring with a mix of blood, fish, and bone. Prune back suckers to control spread
pests & diseases	Capsid bugs could be a problem, so regular checks should be made for even the slightest damage

❄ *very hardy*

❄ Araucaria araucana
Monkey Puzzle Tree

A very peculiar-looking plant from Chile that people either love passionately or loathe completely. It is totally unlike any other fully hardy tree. Leaves are sharp blades that cover each branch and the length of the trunk, making it impossible to climb, hence its common name. Branches are long and spidery. Cones are sometimes produced on older specimens which contain edible seeds. The timber was once widely used in carpentry. It can eventually reach 60ft (18m) over a period of about 100 years. *A. araucana* was very fashionable in the 19th century, but it is seen less now as fewer gardeners have the patience to grow it. This evergreen conifer is excellent for planting on the coast in exposed positions as it is so wind-resistant.

Monkey puzzles love lots of sunshine and moist, loamy soil. They should be planted where there is plenty of space around them to appreciate their beautiful shape. This is not a tree that can be moved easily if it is found to be growing in the wrong place. Plant one that is at least 2ft (60cm) tall, although this will be fairly costly and mature thirty-year-old trees can be prohibitively expensive. An annual feed of blood, fish, and bone would be beneficial, especially to young plants. A couple of handfuls should be sprinkled around the base in mid-spring. This is a very variable plant, as groupings of the plant will show. In any group of *Araucaria araucana*, it would be difficult to find two that are identical.

Araucaria araucana

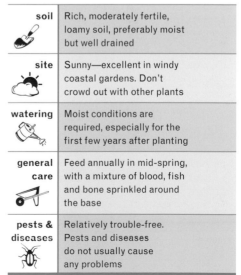

Araucaria araucana

soil	Rich, moderately fertile, loamy soil, preferably moist but well drained
site	Sunny—excellent in windy coastal gardens. Don't crowd out with other plants
watering	Moist conditions are required, especially for the first few years after planting
general care	Feed annually in mid-spring, with a mixture of blood, fish and bone sprinkled around the base
pests & diseases	Relatively trouble-free. Pests and diseases do not usually cause any problems

❄ *very hardy*

❄ Arbutus x andrachnoides

Red-Barked Strawberry Tree

This tree is almost total perfection. Its long list of attributes would start with its elegant, finely serrated leaves that mass together to form a dense head of foliage. It has amazing cinnamon-red wood that peels from the branches and trunk in strips throughout the year. It has large clusters of white, waxy, bell-shaped flowers throughout most of the winter. It is evergreen, easy to grow, fast growing when young, will tolerate poor chalky soil, is happy in exposed positions, is resistant to drought, has attractive bright green spring growth, and, as well as all this, is a manageable size for a small garden as it is unlikely to exceed 25ft (8m) even after several decades. As this is a hybrid, it is sterile, so the strawberry-type fruits will appear only rarely, unlike the common Strawberry tree (*Arbutus unedo*), which is one of its parents.

When planting, choose a site that is within easy reach, as the bark is so beautiful after a shower of rain that people usually want to touch it. Staking for at least the first two years is vital (see pages 14–15 for the correct way of doing this). Also, buy a decent-sized tree with some visible red bark to

Arbutus x andrachnoides

ensure that the correct plant has been acquired. These trees are notorious for being wrongly labeled. Be sure that your nursery is stocking the right plant before you make your purchase.

soil	Will tolerate poor, even chalky soil, as long as it is well drained
site	Sunny position, preferably sheltered from very strong winds
watering	Plenty for the first couple of years until drought-resistance develops
general care	Feed annually in spring. Dropping of older leaves occurs early spring. This should last for 3–4 weeks
pests & diseases	Black fungal spots develop on the foliage if the plant is waterlogged or confined to a pot for too long

Arbutus x andrachnoides

 hardy

❄ Azara microphylla

A beautiful weeping tree with lots of tiny, glossy leaves cascading from delicate branches. This graceful, evergreen tree brings a touch of elegance to even the smallest garden. After as long as ten years, it is unlikely to be more than 12–15ft (4m). Like so many excellent plants, it comes from Chile. It is tough and hardy in many colder climates. In severe winters, it can be cut back to the ground by frost, but nearly always recovers to regain its former glory. The *pièce de résistance* of *A. microphylla* is the incredible vanilla fragrance that oozes from its almost microscopic yellow flowers during early spring. Its powerful scent can be enjoyed from many feet away and a small garden can easily be flooded with its delightful perfume.

The soil should be moist and fertile. Too much sun will give the leaves a yellow tinge and too much shade will make the crown rather thin. To keep the growth dense and the foliage dark and glossy, light shade is best. Shelter from strong winds is desirable, although the odd salty blast from coastal breezes will be fine. Although not a lime-hater, thin, chalky soil should be avoided unless constant watering and feeding can be provided. If left to grow naturally, it develops into a large shrub. Removing lower branches as it grows will turn it into a single-stemmed tree instead, which is a much more shapely option.

Azara microphylla

Azara microphylla

soil		Light, manure-enriched, free-draining soil gives the best results
site		Light shade is best, with shelter for protection against very strong winds
watering		Needs constant moisture, particularly during early growth period
general care		An annual dose of blood, fish, and bone in spring. Saw off lower branches to create a tree rather than a shrub
pests & diseases		Relatively trouble-free. Pests and diseases do not usually cause any problems

❄ *hardy*

❄ Cordyline australis
New Zealand Cabbage Palm

A fine example of exotica, despite being neither a cabbage nor a palm, as its common name suggests. This is a fast-growing tree that has become much more widely planted in the last few years, partly because it is better known, but also due to the milder winters that have been experienced in many places during the last decade. Corky trunks are topped with a bushy head of long, narrow leaves that are very tolerant of salty winds, making it an excellent choice for a seaside garden. Flowers are large, white clusters that smell exquisite—the fragrance can waft across the air and be detected from considerable distances away. After flowering, the head of foliage will divide into two or three branches, eventually building up into huge masses. Trees can reach 15–20ft (5–6m) and be grown as either single or multistemmed plants. The variegated form *C. australis* 'Albertii' is often available, although the green variety is far superior and much hardier. There are also many red forms to be found. These are all utterly repellent(!), with names such as 'Purple Tower'. Nearly all will die within two years or revert to an unpleasant muddy brown color.

C. australis is commonly seen growing in pots as part of a summer bedding scheme. They are suitable for pots for one season only and should then be planted into the ground. Regular brown-bitting is required to keep it looking cared-for. Step-by-step details of brown-bitting are provided on pages 22–23. It is frequently found wrongly labeled as *Dracaena indivisa*.

Cordyline australis

Cordyline australis

soil		Good quality loam is preferred, but generally not too fussy
site		Sun or light shade. Good tree for exposed, windy gardens
watering		Well-drained soil essential. Too much moisture will rot the roots, causing collapse
general care		Winter wrapping from mid-winter until early spring should be considered (see pages 20–21)
pests & diseases		Usually fairly trouble-free outside. Red spider mite is a frequent pest on plants grown in conservatories

❄ *tender*

❄ Cupressus sempervirens 'Pyramidalis'

Italian Cypress

A familiar sight to anyone visiting Tuscany, this distinctive tree immediately conjures up pictures of the Mediterranean. The 'Pyramidalis' form is an extra narrow version of Italian cypress, generally growing to no more than 18in (45cm) wide at the base and narrowing to a point at the top. After twenty years, the height could be 30ft (9m). They are reputed to be tender, but this is not so. Their reputation for being otherwise dates back to 1684 when many were killed in one of the coldest winters on record. Since that date, they have survived many severe winters without any problems

soil	Should be poor and well drained. Acid or alkaline soil is acceptable. Do not feed
site	Thrives in full sun in a position that is sheltered from strong winds
watering	Newly planted trees must be watered regularly until established
general care	Regular clipping during spring and summer seasons, as described in more detail in the text
pests & diseases	Aphids followed by sooty mold can be a problem. Buy trees labeled as resistant to Coryneum disease

Cupressus sempervirens 'Pyramidalis'

at all. The wood and crushed foliage give off a lovely pungent aroma and an essential oil can be distilled from the shoots. Apart from 'Pyramidalis', these trees sometimes have names like 'Stricta', 'Green pencil', or 'Totem'. They are all a narrow form of *C. sempervirens*.

Newly planted trees must be regularly watered for the first couple of years, but once established, they are outstandingly drought-resistant. They are not good in windy positions, and exposed coastal sites should be avoided rather than to try and stake them upright. Poor soil is preferred to keep the new growth stunted and stubby. Too much food produces long, lax growth which makes the tree look scruffy and in need of more frequent clipping. This should be done regularly with ordinary garden shears over its entire length during spring and summer. The more often this is done, the denser the foliage will be, just like a hedge. The height can be restricted by chopping off the top at a slanting angle, never straight across as this would result in a very unnatural-looking tree.

Horse chestnut-type cones are often produced in large numbers. These should be cut off as their weight can pull the branches out of shape.

❄ *very hardy*

❄ Eriobotrya japonica

The Loquat

Given the right conditions, this jungly evergreen plant can develop impressive-looking leaves up to 2ft (60cm) long. Each leaf is deeply crinkled and rather solid. The deep green color is dusted with a powdery coating making them similar to some of the large-leafed species of rhododendron. *E. japonica* grows naturally as a large 13–16ft (4–5m) shrub, but with careful pruning can easily be coaxed into a splendid little single-stemmed tree. Fragrant flowers are produced in late summer but these can coincide with the first frosts and are therefore killed off. In warmer gardens, where the flowers survive, these can be followed by large, fat, apricot fruits if the summer has been especially hot. These

Eriobotrya japonica

Eriobotrya japonica

are edible but the birds usually get there first. The new spring growth is extremely attractive, imitating fresh green shuttlecocks.

To get the very best out of this magnificent-looking plant, feeding with well-rotted manure accompanied by copious amounts of water will be necessary. Although quite happy in the sun, to get the maximum-sized foliage, shade is a must—the more shade, the bigger the leaves. If left as a shrub, make sure there is plenty of space for it to grow—a width of 10ft (3m) is not unusual. If grown as a tree, remove any suckers as soon as they appear and gradually cut away lower branches as required. This plant can take severe pruning if it outgrows its allocated space. Pruning should be done in spring just as the new growth starts. Pruning in the fall is not a good idea, as the plant can "sulk" all through the winter before recovering the following year. Late frosts can blacken new growth. If this happens, just cut it off—more will soon appear again. In mid-spring, just before the new leaves appear, alarming amounts of old foliage can be shed. As the leaves are so large, this is very noticeable. Piles of yellow leaves form quite a heap but this is all quite normal. New leaves soon take their place and the whole nasty experience quickly becomes a distant memory.

soil	Grow in manure-enriched, moist, fertile soil that drains well
site	Preferably shade in a sheltered spot as wind can tear the leaves
watering	Copious amounts are required all through the growing season
general care	Feed in mid-spring and early summer, either with manure or else a mixture of blood, fish, and bone
pests & diseases	Check new growth for aphids. Leaf spot can be a problem; remove infected leaves immediately

❄ *hardy*

✳ Eucalyptus aggregata

The Black Gum

The perfect tree to form a screen, *E. aggregata* is by far the fastest-growing plant in this book. Height could easily reach 30ft (9m) in six years and the head of foliage is dense enough to give privacy without blocking out all the light. Leaves are long, narrow, and glaucous-green, and when they are crushed, they emit the familiar aromatic eucalyptus scent. The bark is constantly changing its appearance as small areas peel off, leaving patches of different shades of brown and gray.

A sunny position is best with fairly poor, sandy soil if possible. If the soil is too rich, the growth above ground becomes too fast for the root system to support its weight, the result being that a strong gale or storm could easily blow it over unless it has been strongly supported with tree stakes when first planted. Unlike most eucalyptus trees, *E. aggregata* is happy to receive constant and copious amounts of water. It can even grow in a permanently boggy position. Another of its characteristics, not shared with many other Gum trees, is its ability to cope with alkaline conditions,

soil	Poor, neutral to acid soil is preferred, although some lime or chalk is acceptable
site	Sunny but sheltered spot is best. Windy, exposed sites tolerated if heavily staked
watering	Almost impossible to overwater, but can also cope with near-drought conditions
general care	Virtually maintenance-free. Remove lower branches if a single-stemmed tree is required
pests & diseases	Once planted out, this tree usually remains untroubled by pests and diseases

Eucalyptus aggregata

Eucalyptus aggregata

although excessively chalky ground is best avoided.

E. aggregata grows naturally as a multistemmed tree, and its spread can almost equal its height. This is fine for large gardens, but not practical for smaller ones. Instead, train it as a single-stemmed specimen by removing the lower branches gradually until all branches and leaves are above head height. This allows people to walk underneath it, and the only space taken up in the garden is the diameter of the trunk.

✳ *very hardy*

Eucalyptus niphophila 'Debeuzevillei'

Jounama
Snow Gum

There are several Snow gums, but the variety 'Debeuzevillei' is one of the most wonderful. The bark on the trunk and along the branches is a beautiful mixture of different-colored patches ranging from snowy white, pale gray, silvery gray, cream, and palest beige. Leaves are large, leathery, blue-gray, and highly aromatic.

soil	Sandy, well-drained, neutral to acid soil is best. Must be lime-free
site	Full sun in a sheltered position away from any strong winds
watering	Only necessary for newly planted trees. Too much water can damage the roots
general care	More or less maintenance-free. When newly planted, stakes are a good option to support fast-growing foliage
pests & diseases	Once planted out, this variety usually has few problems with pests and diseases

Eucalyptus niphophila 'Debeuzevillei'

Eucalyptus niphophila 'Debeuzevillei'

This tree is much smaller than many hardy Gum trees, reaching a height of only 25ft (8m) in a temperate climate and taking at least ten years to grow this tall, making it the best variety of eucalyptus for small gardens. It can be left as a large multistemmed bush, but is perfectly suitable for training as a single-stemmed tree simply by removing all lower branches as required. It makes an excellent choice as a specimen feature if there is only room in the garden for one special evergreen tree.

Full sun is essential and sandy, well-drained, neutral to acid soil is best. If the soil is rich and fertile, it is recommended to stake this tree heavily when it is first planted, so that the fast-growing crown of foliage can be fully supported. Otherwise, it can become top-heavy before the roots have had a chance to burrow down deep enough to anchor it during heavy gales or storms. Apart from this, it is a very easy tree to cultivate and the only way it can usually be killed is by keeping the roots too wet.

very hardy

✳ Ficus carica

The Common Fig

Although *F. carica* is commonly seen spread-eagled against a sunny wall, it is for its fruit that it is usually planted. It is rarely grown for its superb architectural qualities, which is a pity because it blends in beautifully with exotic planting schemes if planted and grown as a proper tree. It is slow-growing, but can eventually develop into a fat, stocky tree with lovely silvery-gray bark, topped with copious amounts of enormous, lobed leaves, which turn a rich butter-yellow in the fall. On hot sunny days, the leaves can give off a very pleasant aroma. The fact that it is deciduous is a slight disappointment, but it more than makes up for this by its valuable presence in the garden during summer and fall. Height at maturity is unlikely to exceed 16ft (5m).

Unless grown under glass or in a mild garden, the fruit can often be an unrewarding experience, so the method of cultivation given here is to produce

Trees

soil	Rich, moist, and fertile conditions will give the best results
site	A sheltered spot in the shade— the more shade, the bigger the leaves
watering	Water regularly. Although drought-resistant, prefers moist, but never boggy, conditions
general care	Prune back hard each year when the tree is dormant—fall (or spring, if in a cold area) is a good time
pests & diseases	Capsid bug can disfigure the leaves. Coral spot is sometimes a problem on older plants

a fine-looking foliage plant. Any fruit produced in the process should be considered as an added extra. With this in mind, the instructions here are more or less the opposite to those found in other books. Fertile, deeply cultivated soil, enriched annually with lots of manure and grown in a shady position in the ground (not in a pot) will give very rewarding results. Water regularly until established. *F. carica* is often sold in very small containers to restrict the root growth, which traditionally aids fruit production. Plant into the ground at the first available opportunity—its huge sigh of relief at being out of the pot will be almost deafening!

Pruning is an important part of the care for *Ficus carica*. It can be done for a variety of reasons: if the tree has been planted in a small garden, pruning can be done in order to keep it a manageable size; pruning the crown can help to keep it a tidy shape; hard pruning each year will ensure that the following season's foliage grows to its maximum size; and, finally, any overlapping branches that are crowded together can be removed to create a more pleasing shape. Fall is a good time for any pruning to be carried out— unless you live in a very cold area, in which case wait until the spring. Pruning should always be done when the tree is dormant, after the leaves have dropped.

Ficus carica

✳ *very hardy*

❄ Genista aetnensis

Mount Etna Broom

A small decorative evergreen tree with a distinctive weeping habit that grows to no more than around 16ft (5m), making it a possible contender for even the most compact garden. Foliage is very sparse, but the branches are light and feathery, almost like green wispy grass, giving the whole tree a delicate look. Despite its frail appearance, however, it is exceptionally hardy. The trunk can become gnarled and twisted when mature and is rarely straight. In mid-summer, the entire head is covered with a mass of loud, bright yellow flowers that are highly fragrant on a sunny day. It is also wind-resistant and therefore makes an excellent choice for a coastal garden. As with most members of the Leguminosae family, this is a fast-growing plant and easy to cultivate. Choose a tree that is at least five years old, as they can look rather unexciting until they reach this age.

Full sun is vital and soil must be very well drained. Once established, it will grow on the poorest, driest, stoniest soil

imaginable with almost no assistance. It has an exceptionally high resistance to drought. Acid, neutral, or chalky soils are all suitable. It is important to stake *G. aetnensis* at the time of planting as it can take a few years for the trunk to increase its girth sufficiently to become self-supporting. If left to grow naturally, it develops into a large shrub. Persuade it to become a tree by regularly removing the lower branches until the desired length of trunk has been achieved. Pruning the crown lightly each year can give it a bushier appearance. No other maintenance is required. This is a very easy tree to cultivate, even annual feeding can be dispensed with.

Genista aetnensis

soil	Any—poor to moderately fertile—as long as it is well drained
site	Full sun—especially suitable for exposed gardens
watering	Water well until established, then irrigation can virtually be ignored
general care	Maintenance-free. Light annual pruning if desired. Branches on very old trees occasionally need support
pests & diseases	Relatively trouble-free. Pests and diseases do not usually cause any problems

❄ *very hardy*

75

Laurus nobilis angustifolia

Narrow-Leafed Bay

Much less well known than the more commonly grown Bay tree, which is a pity because in many ways it is much more desirable. The foliage is a fresher green and more attractive, having gracefully elongated leaves that are slightly serrated. They still have the familiar aromatic scent when crushed, and can be used just as successfully for culinary purposes. Other advantages that this variety has over ordinary Bay trees are, firstly, its extra resilience to salty winds, making it more suitable for coastal gardens and, secondly, it is considerably hardier, so that it can be grown in much colder gardens.

L. nobilis angustifolia can be left as a large shrub or grown into a small tree. It generally grows to no more than 16ft (5m) taking fifteen years to do so, making it an ideal evergreen tree for a small space. Just as the common Bay tree is often found clipped into small lollipop shapes or cones and growing in pots either side of the front door, this tree can be treated in exactly the same way. Clipping into shape should start when the plant is young and be done little and often throughout the growing season.

soil	Any soil, although one that is reasonably rich and well drained would be preferred
site	Full sun or light shade. Happy in either sheltered or exposed gardens
watering	Water frequently for the first couple of seasons until drought-tolerance develops
general care	An annual feed with a few handfuls of a blood, fish, and bone mix around the base in mid-spring is beneficial
pests & diseases	Scale insect is a familiar visitor and must be dealt with at the first sign. Scrape off immediately

Laurus nobilis angustifolia

Laurus nobilis angustifolia

L

Trees

❄ *very hardy*

❄ Ligustrum lucidum

Chinese Privet

Fantastic evergreen tree from China with a shapely rounded head. *L. lucidum* is fast growing, quickly reaching 12ft (4m) and ultimately approaching around 25ft (8m) maximum. It is a wonderful street tree, very tolerant of pollution. Left to its own devices, it can grow as a large shrub, but it is much more handsome if grown as a tree with a clear stem of at least 6–7ft (2m). Leaves are large and glossy, and masses of frothy, fragrant white flowers are produced in late summer, followed by clusters of blue-black fruits in late fall. Its wind-tolerance is surprisingly good for a large-leafed tree.

Ligustrum lucidum

L. lucidum needs plenty of space around it so that its architectural shape can be fully appreciated. Any soil will do—although it is particularly happy on chalk. To keep the head tight and bushy, full sun or light shade is preferred. It will have a much more open habit in a shady spot. It is a very easy tree to grow, requiring virtually no maintenance. When first planted, some initial support will be needed and a strong tree stake should be used for at least two or three years. Cats seem to delight in gouging great furrows down the bark of this tree, so wrap a rabbit guard around the trunk. It is often confused with *L. japonicum* and is sometimes labeled incorrectly at nurseries.

	soil	Tolerates any soil type, as long as it is well drained. Particularly happy in chalk.
	site	Happy anywhere—but the sunnier the spot, the denser the foliage
	watering	Appreciates lots of moisture, especially for the first two seasons after planting
	general care	A few generous handfuls of blood, fish, and bone around the base in mid-spring gives excellent results
	pests & diseases	Generally trouble-free from pests and diseases, although watch out for cats scratching the bark!

Ligustrum lucidum

❄ *very hardy*

Lyonothamnus floribundus aspleniifolius

Catalina Ironwood

An utterly beautiful evergreen tree that has soft ferny leaves, dark red craggy bark, and a ridiculously long name. It is a fast-growing, conical-shaped tree, and in the United States, its native country, it can reach 16ft (5m) in five years. Elsewhere, its ultimate height is unlikely to exceed 25ft (8m). The leaves are bright green and rough to the touch. When the weather is either dry and frosty or extremely hot and sunny, the foliage gives off a pleasant marshmallow aroma. In its early years, all the energy seems to go into reaching a good height. The bark does not develop its gnarled rugged look for several years. When first planted at Kew Gardens, London, in around 1900, it attracted much attention for "the beauty of its fern-like leaves, its luxuriance, and graceful habit." The creamy white flowers appear only on mature specimens after a very warm summer.

This tree, lovely as it may be, is a bit of a fusspot. It must have lots of sun, shelter from cold winds, very well-drained soil, and a mild location. The protection of a warm

Lyonothamnus floribundus aspleniifolius

Lyonothamnus floribundus aspleniifolius

soil	Neutral to acid preferred. Tolerates alkaline soil if lime content is not excessive
site	Full sun in a sheltered spot. In frost-prone areas, shelter from cold, drying winds
watering	Water regularly for first few seasons. Once established, irrigation unnecessary
general care	Responds well to light pruning. A mix of blood, fish, and bone each spring should keep it looking healthy
pests & diseases	Relatively trouble-free, so long as it is planted in the ground and not confined to a pot

and sunny wall would be ideal. Once established it is very drought-resistant. The support of a strong stake when newly planted is essential, and will be needed for at least three years.

hardy

❄ Magnolia grandiflora
Bull Bay

Traditionally seen growing as a large wall shrub, it is far superior if grown as a free-standing plant. This magnificent evergreen tree has huge leaves that are dark green and glossy on the surface and dusted reddish-brown underneath. The flowers are stupendous—massive cream cups up to 1ft (30cm) across with the typical heavily fragrant magnolia scent that can waft around the entire garden from mid-summer until early fall. Each flower lasts only a few days, but mature trees produce a continuous supply for many weeks. Away from their native country, ultimate height will probably be no more than 30ft (9m).

M. grandiflora is perfectly hardy, although when first introduced, its exotic good looks

	soil	Unusually unfussy for a Magnolia—will even grow on alkaline soil
	site	Full sun or light shade in a sheltered position is preferred
	watering	Appreciates adequate moisture, but cannot cope with a boggy site
	general care	Feed well with blood, fish, and bone in mid-spring. Pruning can be ruthless. Branches can be cut back in mid-spring
	pests & diseases	Relatively trouble-free. Pests and diseases do not usually cause any problems

M

Trees

Magnolia grandiflora

led gardeners to assume that it could not possibly be so. This is why plants were always given the protection of a warm wall. They can be trained into large conical bushes with regular pruning or as proper trees by removing the lower branches. Pruning can be ruthless if desired. Branches can be cut back savagely in mid-spring, but don't worry—these will recover reasonably well later the same year. This savage pruning will be rewarded by the end of the following year with stunning results. Thick, luscious growth of wonderful new foliage will cover the whole plant. Keep an eye on the appearance of the leaves. If the soil is exceptionally alkaline, they will take on

a yellowish tinge. This can be remedied with a few doses of sequestered iron.

Propagation is best tried from cuttings, as seed-grown plants can take many years to flower. Another method of propagating to try is layering, where a stem is pegged to the soil, and stays attached to the parent plant until rooting is induced. However, this method works only on young, nonwoody growth.

Various named forms of this plant—such as 'Exmouth', 'Goliath', 'Ferruginea', or 'Samuel Somer'—are occasionally offered for sale. Delightful as they all are for their variations of leaf type or flower size, the straight form of *M. grandiflora* is by far the hardiest, easiest, and most widely available. It is a perfectly acceptable variety, except perhaps to the most serious of magnolia collectors.

Magnolia grandiflora

❄ *very hardy*

✳ Myrtus luma

(syn.
Luma apiculata)
Orange
Bark Myrtle

The soft suede-like orange bark makes this tree irresistible to the touch. Its color varies in intensity throughout the year. During the summer, the bark splits and peels to reveal patches of creamy white, which gradually darken and change back to orange again. Young plants do not have the characteristic orange bark. This will start to appear after about five years. The foliage is a dense mass of tiny, evergreen leaves that are aromatic when crushed. Fragrant white flowers appear from mid-summer until mid-fall, followed by large, fat fruits. These are black, juicy, and edible. *M. luma* grows best in high rainfall areas. Away from its native South America, expect an ultimate height of no more than 25ft (8m). This tree has been reliably reported as being able to grow in bogs, which explains why copious amounts of water are so necessary to produce good results.

This tree has a variety of different names and can appear on plant lists as *M. apiculata*, *Eugenia apiculata*, or even *Myrceugenia apiculata,* to name just a few. The name I have elected to use, *Myrtus luma*, is the easiest. A variegated form is also available, which is smaller, less hardy, and much less pleasing to the eye.

soil	Most soil types are suitable, but happiest in well-drained and fertile conditions
site	Grows well in sun or shade in a sheltered spot away from cold winds
watering	*M. luma* is extremely intolerant of drought, so needs constant irrigation
general care	Feed just enough to keep the foliage a good dark green color. It is a good candidate for topiary
pests & diseases	This species is not prone to any particular pest or disease and is usually trouble-free

Myrtus luma

Myrtus luma

✳ *hardy*

❄ Olea europea
Olive Tree

A tree usually associated with only the warmest of European countries. However, this tough tree can adapt to many less favorable climates if either given the protection of a sunny wall in a mild garden, or grown in sheltered coastal areas. This small, spreading tree could reach up to 20ft (6m) tall and 16ft (4m) across when mature. Foliage is thick enough to create a bit of privacy, but sparse enough not to block out the light. Leaves are gray-green and the tree trunks are rarely straight, but gnarled, twisting, and very shapely. Flowers are small insignificant clusters of pale yellow. In cooler climates, fruits are unlikely and if they do form, would probably never ripen unless the summer has been exceptionally hot.

Apart from the limited hardiness of this tree, *O. europea* is very easy to cultivate. Although commonly seen growing in poor soil on hillsides in Italy and Spain, where it is planted solely for the olive crop, much better results can be achieved from the foliage if planted in richer, loamy, well-drained soil. A light feed of blood, fish, and bone once a year around mid-spring would also be beneficial to this tree.

Once established, even extreme drought can be coped with. Never plant in ground where flooding or boggy conditions are likely as this will result in certain death. In colder climates, where it is not possible to leave it outside all winter, growing it in a large pot is a possible alternative. It is quite a good candidate for this and will live happily in a pot for years if the size is controlled by regular pruning. One thing that is often overlooked, however, is a container-grown plant's need for plenty of water during the summer. Watering once a day in hot weather is often necessary and the roots should never be allowed to dry out. Apart from this, *O. europea* is one of the most suitable plants there is for conservatories as it rarely gets pests or diseases (*see* table for possible unwanted visitors), and can cope very well with hot dry atmospheres. Propagation from cuttings is surprisingly easy.

Olea europea

soil	Rich, loamy, well-drained soil is preferred, although it can tolerate poor soil
site	Full sun in a mild, sheltered garden. Grows well in a pot if pruned regularly
watering	Once established, very little is required unless grown in a pot
general care	A light mix of blood, fish, and bone in mid-spring is beneficial. Prune between spring and summer if required
pests & diseases	Rarely a problem. If this tree is grown under glass, make occasional inspections for scale insect

❄ *tender*

❄ Paulownia tomentosa
The Foxglove Tree

Depending on how you choose to grow it, *P. tomentosa* can have two very different and very distinctive looks. Firstly, by leaving it to grow naturally, it will develop into a small tree reaching no more than around 25ft (8m) in an average garden. The bark is attractively spotted and speckled. Branches form a neat, open canopy and the flowers are borne in late spring, before the leaves start to appear. They are fragrant, pinkish-purple, and shaped like a foxglove flower. Trees covered in these early blooms look almost tropical. Leaves start to unfurl in late spring. These are large and soft, heart-shaped, and very jungly. Although this tree is totally hardy, flowers are only reliably produced in warmer areas. The buds start to form in the fall and a hard winter can kill them off before they have a chance to open up.

The second method of growing *P. tomentosa* is much more dramatic and extremely good fun. Instead of allowing it to become a proper tree, chop it down hard

soil	Rich, fertile, and well-drained soil is preferred for this tree
site	Light shade is best in a sheltered position as wind can tear the large leaves
watering	Copious amounts are needed during the growing season
general care	Feed heavily every four weeks from mid-spring until mid-summer. This should be watered in well
pests & diseases	Capsid bugs can unfortunately be a menace, tearing unsightly holes into the large leaves

Paulownia tomentosa

Paulownia tomentosa

to within a few inches of old wood each year in early spring. Although this prevents it from flowering, compensation is given in the form of leaves that can reach gigantic proportions of almost 2½ft (75cm) across. The whole plant can reach a height of 10ft (3m) each year before cutting it back down to start the whole process over again. When the leaves drop in the fall, their size makes them land with an audible thud as they hit the ground.

❄ *very hardy*

❄ Phillyrea latifolia

This beautiful little tree was regularly planted at the beginning of the 1900s and is often seen in churchyards. It seemed to go out of fashion fifty years later and is long overdue for a revival. The trunk is rarely straight, but twisted and gnarled like its cousin, the European olive. The foliage is a series of tightly packed heads sculpted into domes and billowing cloud shapes. Its ultimate height of around 25ft (8m) is usually matched by its width so lots of space around it is necessary to appreciate the architectural outline. *P. latifolia* is very slow-growing and does not start to develop its characteristic shape for at least five years. As with many evergreens, it is best seen in the winter when most other plants near it have dropped their leaves. Insignificant clusters of greenish flowers appear in late spring, sometimes followed by spherical blue-black fruits during warm summers. It is hardy almost anywhere, provided that it receives shelter from cold winds.

Phillyrea latifolia

Phillyrea latifolia

P. *latifolia* has the appearance of a miniature Holm Oak (see page 89) and is ideal for small gardens. They are particularly suited to Japanese-style gardens and also make a wonderful choice for planting as an evergreen avenue. This is a very unfussy tree that is easy to grow. It is just as happy in woodland as it is in a small suburban garden, or indeed coastal surroundings, because of its tolerance to salty winds. When first planted, it is best to stake it well. A few handfuls of blood, fish, and bone can be sprinkled around its base in mid-spring, particularly if the soil is very poor. If it is grown as a tree, remove any epicormic growth (shoots that sprout from the trunk).

soil	A very unfussy tree. Grows happily in any well-drained soil
site	Sun or shade. Happy in woodland areas, suburban and coastal gardens
watering	Water well for first few seasons, then it becomes very drought-resistant
general care	Feeding not usually necessary unless soil is very poor. Stake well when first planted
pests & diseases	Rarely a problem, although newly bought plants should be checked for whitefly if grown under glass

Trees

P

❄ *very hardy*

❄ Pinus patula

Mexican Yellow Pine

A large, spreading tree that needs plenty of space around it to appreciate the long flowing lines of the branches. In its native country of Mexico, *P. patula* can quickly grow to gigantic proportions, but even in colder climates 30ft (9m) can be attained in ten years, ultimately reaching 50ft (15m) tall if left unchecked. Branches start low down and almost drape the ground. They have a wide spread of at least 20ft (6m) from tip to tip and hang gracefully in layers all the way up the tree. From each branch, elegant long needles of a brilliant emerald green are suspended, giving a very shaggy effect—almost like a green orangutan. The trunk is attractive in its own right, being a craggy reddish-brown, but this is nearly always hidden by the thick foliage.

soil	Very well-drained, loamy soil is preferred for this particular pine
site	Position in full sun in a sheltered position away from cold winds
watering	Hates boggy conditions, but water regularly until established
general care	Occasional light feed. Give a blood, fish, and bone mix in late spring if needed. Feed only when tree is actively growing
pests & diseases	Pests and diseases are not usually a problem as long as the soil is well drained

Pinus patula

It is reputed to be a lime-hater, but experience has proved this not to be so, if the lime content is not too excessive. What this tree hates most of all is strong, cold winds, which will turn the tips of the leaves brown. It also performs very badly in shade, resulting in a drawn, open habit. Pruning can be done to reduce the height and width considerably if it is carried out early on in its life and given regular trimming throughout the growing season. This can give it a Japanese-style look like a large bonsai. If trees like this are required, they are best bought that way to start with, so that pruning can be continued in the same manner, without specialist knowledge being so necessary. However, this is such a beautiful tree, it is better to give it enough space to allow it to mature naturally.

Pinus patula

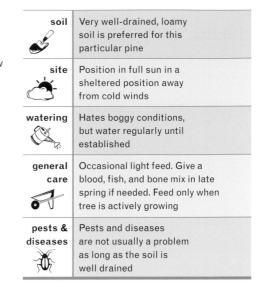

❄ *hardy*

❋ Pinus pinea
Umbrella Pine
or Stone Pine

Shapely, round-headed evergreen tree ideal for medium-sized gardens requiring more than a hint of the Mediterranean. *P. pinea* planted together with *Cupressus sempervirens* reflect the Tuscan flavor brilliantly. This tree's height eventually matches the width of its head, which will be around 16ft (5m) after fifteen years, so plenty of space must be left around it to appreciate its spherical symmetry. The trunk is rough and craggy, and can become fairly stocky after just a few years. The head of foliage is a mass of soft, feathery pine needles. Large cones are regularly produced, which contain edible seeds sold as pine nuts.

This tree is perfect for growing in all sorts of hostile environments. Poor, dry, sandy soil is not a problem and it copes very well with strong coastal winds. Good results will be obtained whether the site is on clay, flint, chalk, or loam. *P. pinea* is suitable for planting as a single specimen or in small groves. They also make splendid avenues. Strong tree stakes will be required when planting and should be kept in place for

at least three years. Don't feed for several years unless the soil is really poor. This is to ensure that all the energy will be concentrated on the root system of the tree, which needs to be strong to support the wide crown of foliage.

P. pinea will never thrive in boggy conditions, although it should be kept regularly watered for the first two seasons until the tree has become established. Drought-tolerance begins to develop as the roots grow down far enough to find their own water supply. To get the roots off to a good start, introduce a few handfuls of bonemeal to the planting hole. If large, container-grown trees are being planted, considerable leaf drop should be expected during its first year. This is all as a result of the tree being transplanted and going into shock. By the following season, growth should be lush and plentiful once more.

Pinus pinea

soil	Grows well whether in clay, flint, chalk, loam, or even poor, sandy soil
site	Full sun. Copes particularly well with strong coastal winds
watering	Hates boggy conditions, but water for first two seasons until well established
general care	Gradually saw off the lower branches to raise the crown and keep the head a good round shape
pests & diseases	Pests and diseases are not usually a problem for this particular species of pine

❋ *very hardy*

❄ Podocarpus salignus

Willowleaf Podocarp

Only the most hard-hearted of gardeners would fail to go weak at the knees at the sight of this luscious tree. Shaggy heaps of luxurious, emerald green, willow-like foliage make this beautiful evergreen conifer one of the most essential additions to any garden, especially one with exotic tendencies. Although *P. salignus* can reach lofty heights in its native country, away from Chile it can realistically be expected to reach only 26ft (5m), and that height will take at least twenty years to attain. It is much hardier than generally described and can survive severe winters if grown in a protected spot sheltered from cold winds. Although the bark is usually hidden behind the dense foliage, it is attractive in its own right, being reddish-brown, fibrous, and peeling off in strips. Small red berries are occasionally produced. These will look familiar and act as a reminder that it is related to the Common yew (*Taxus baccata*).

P. salignus prefers to be grown away from other plants as it does not like to compete for food and moisture. It is very slow to establish, taking up to two years for the roots to settle in before any sign of growth commences. After that, new foliage is produced at a rate of around 6–9in (15–20cm) each year. Plenty of moisture is essential and a position in light shade is best. The color of the leaves is much more attractive away from direct sunlight. Pruning is not necessary unless a hedge or smaller plant is required. Clipping should be done little and often, so that only the new growth is shaped. Cutting into old wood should be avoided. Lower branches can be removed to expose more of the lovely bark, but choosing to cut off such beautiful foliage can be difficult to justify. Apart from a light feed in late spring, make sure that the tree is not overfed, as too much food can scorch the ends of the leaves.

Podocarpus salignus

soil	Neutral to acid preferred, although alkaline conditions can be coped with fairly well
site	A sheltered spot in light shade is best, away from other trees and plants
watering	The best results are produced by watering regularly enough to keep the soil moist but not boggy
general care	A light mix of blood, fish, and bone can be given in late spring. Too much food can scorch the ends of the leaves
pests & diseases	Generally, this particular tree is refreshingly free from blight by pests and diseases

❄ *very hardy*

Pseudopanax crassifolius

The Lancewood

A real horticultural oddity, being one of the strangest-looking trees you are likely to encounter. The trunk and branches are craggy but dead straight, and they were used by the Maori fraternity of New Zealand for making lances and spear handles, hence the common name. It is for the leaves that this tree is considered peculiar. They undergo metamorphosis through several stages, the second stage being the oddest. The leaves are up to 2ft (60cm) long, only ½in (1cm) wide, almost black, and look as if they are made of plastic. Sometimes they have an orange or red stripe running down

soil	Any soil type. Thrives in a large pot, but best if planted directly into the ground
site	Full sun in a quiet, sheltered spot. Does not cope well when buffeted by sea winds
watering	Happy in dry conditions. Requires regular watering if grown in a container
general care	No special care needed. However, may need restrictive pruning if kept under glass
pests & diseases	Aphids are often a problem on new shoots, but generally trouble-free from pests and diseases

Pseudopanax crassifolius

the center. The edges are sharply serrated. Even odder than their appearance is the way they hang downward at an angle of 45°, giving the tree an upside down look to it. Several phases then follow until the leaves reach adulthood. With each stage, the leaves become shorter, wider, and greener until eventually they look almost normal. They also stop hanging down vertically, gradually lifting upward. A mature tree can reach around 20ft (6m) with a crown of evergreen foliage spreading to only 8ft (2.5m) across. The older foliage eventually drops off, hiding all the evidence that once pointed to it being rather unusual. *P. crassifolius* is a tree that is either loved passionately or loathed because it looks so strange. It always seems to get a lot of attention from neighbors.

This tree appears to have an almost nonexistent root system, which makes it an exceptionally good candidate for growing in a large pot, where it can sit happily for years. However, as with all plants, the best results will be gained by planting directly into the soil. It needs a quiet, sheltered spot in a warm garden to be at its most content. Salty sea air can be coped with well, but constant buffeting by sea winds will make it look miserable.

❄ *hardy*

P

Pseudopanax ferox
The Toothed Lancewood

If the description of the *Pseudopanax crassifolius* on the previous page sounded odd, this tree is an even stranger specimen. The leaves metamorphose through several stages from juvenile to adult, with the second phase again being the most peculiar. Leaves are 18in (45cm) long and just ½in (1cm) wide. They are dark brownish-black and often have a red, yellow, or orange stripe running down the center. The edges are very sharply serrated and the whole leaf looks like a large hacksaw blade. They hang down the tree at an angle of 45° and it would be easy to convince yourself that the tree had been planted the wrong way up! It is thought that the leaves have evolved this way to make them look unappetizing to passing animals, thereby assuring the plant's survival into maturity. It is certainly an interesting theory.

This is an incredibly slow-growing tree that may reach only 2ft (60cm) after five years. Away from its native New Zealand, the ultimate height will probably be around only 13ft (4m). It will sit in a container quite happily for years without getting root-bound. It needs virtually no food, just an occasional handful of blood, fish, and bone every couple of years. The only way to kill this tree is by overwatering. Watering should be done sparingly—just enough to keep the soil moist, but not wet.

Pseudopanax ferox

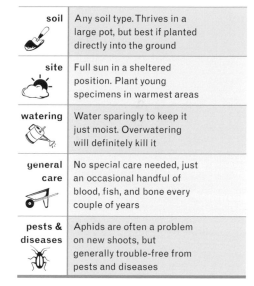

soil	Any soil type. Thrives in a large pot, but best if planted directly into the ground
site	Full sun in a sheltered position. Plant young specimens in warmest areas
watering	Water sparingly to keep it just moist. Overwatering will definitely kill it
general care	No special care needed, just an occasional handful of blood, fish, and bone every couple of years
pests & diseases	Aphids are often a problem on new shoots, but generally trouble-free from pests and diseases

Neighbors seem to delight at poking fun at this wonderfully unusual plant. Because it is so strange-looking, people assume, quite wrongly, that it must be ill or even worse. But learning to feel affection for this tree is not difficult—you really can start to love it in a relatively short time, especially as there is very little in the way of maintenance to keep it happy. Although given the hardiness color code of orange, this applies only to mature plants. Younger specimens should be planted with care in the warmest part of the garden. An occasional once-over to check for aphids on the new shoots is advisable.

Quercus ilex
Holm Oak

Apart from being extremely beautiful, this large evergreen tree is probably one of the most useful and versatile trees available. It can be used as an essential windbreak for all coastal gardens, rarely becoming scorched even after being battered by the most savage salt-laden gales. For smaller coastal gardens, where planting a row of huge trees is impractical, they can be clipped into large hedges instead. Single specimens are sufficiently large enough to impose a majestic presence on any good-sized garden. They can also make the most marvelous avenues if clipped into formal "lollipop" shapes (see below). Mature plants have sturdy gray trunks and are topped with a thick mass of gray-green leaves that shimmer in the breeze. From a distance, the foliage has the appearance of a large olive tree. Although this tree can get enormous, it will take more than fifty years to reach 50ft (15m) tall.

In large gardens, they can have another use. If planted in groves and regularly crown-lifted (crown-lifted means having the lower branches chopped off) they can act as a frost barrier, keeping the temperature of

soil	Will thrive in any soil, even heavy chalk, although loamy soil is best of all	
site	Sun or light shade is preferred, although full shade can be tolerated	
watering	Watering should normally be required only during its first season, unless there is a drought	
general care	Heavily stake newly planted trees. An annual feed of blood, fish, and bone can be given if desired	
pests & diseases	Powdery mildew may be a problem but apart from this, it is generally trouble-free	

the ground underneath higher than it would otherwise be. This means that a wider range of tender exotics could be planted here than in colder, more exposed parts of the garden. For example, for a tree fern, just a couple of degrees of extra warmth could mean the difference between struggling to stay alive as opposed to really thriving.

✻ Trochodendron aralioides

Wheel Tree

A very unusual Japanese tree, the only member of its family, and vaguely related to magnolias. It could be classed either as a large shrub or a small multistemmed tree, rarely getting to more than 20ft (6m) in height if planted outside its native country. The branches spread out widely, and the dimensions of width and height can often be the same. The leaves are waxy in appearance, with scalloped edges, and apple green in color. They are bright pink when still in bud. The flowers are amazing—positively prehistoric-looking things and a bright vivid green. This tree is exceptionally hardy, remaining quite unscathed even after the most severe winters. This can be a difficult plant to get going and should not be planted out if very small. Wait until they are at least 3ft (1m) tall.

Plenty of space is needed around *T. aralioides* for its shape to be fully appreciated. It is very slow-growing and could take up to ten years to reach just 6ft (2m). Because of this, it could be grown quite successfully in a container for a number of years.

During the winter, the foliage can become speckled. These dark brown bits appear to cause no harm at all, and when the plant starts to grow again in the spring, its usual apple green color always seems to come through. Propagation is fairly easy from semi-ripe cuttings taken in late summer, although fresh seed can also be used.

soil	Any fertile soil except for heavy chalk. Can be grown in a container
site	Sun or shade and sheltered from the wind, with plenty of space around it
watering	Prefers a moist situation. Never allow to dry out, especially if grown in a pot
general care	Virtually maintenance-free. Sequestered iron can be added if the soil is excessively alkaline
pests & diseases	Rarely a problem. This tree is usually refreshingly free from blight by pests and diseases

Trochodendron aralioides

✻ *very hardy*

Spiky & Succulent Plants

Many of the spiky plants have such strong shapes that they can be a really bold presence in the garden. There is nothing discreet about them and they are not for the lily-livered! Their spines and thorns are part of their charm, even though they are quite capable of inflicting savage wounds on passers-by. Over the years, regular howls of pain have been heard coming from delivery men having the misfortune to visit my house.

Not only are spiky and succulent plants exceptionally beautiful, their slow rate of growth makes them among the most suitable plants for growing in terracotta pots. Although all plants prefer being in the ground, containers are the only option for roof terraces or for very cold gardens where plants have to be taken inside for the winter. Most of these plants can adapt to desert conditions, however, this does not necessarily mean that this is what they prefer. During the growing season, if these plants are watered regularly, they show their appreciation by growing much faster than they are generally considered capable of doing. The desert regions where many spiky plants come from are based on limestone, which means that they can tolerate soil with a high content of chalk or lime. All in all, these types of plant are very easy to care for.

One thing to remember with fleshy leafed plants is that they are not used to damp, cold, and foggy conditions. They are used to Mexico and Arizona, not Seattle. Although they are occasionally subjected to below freezing temperatures, the air in the desert always stays dry, so they have never had to build up any resistance to fungus attacks and rotting. Therefore, in very cold gardens with a high rainfall, a helping hand is often needed. If, during the fall, a systemic fungicide drench is administered to the leaves and around the base, this will help to fight off many of the problems associated with the cold and wet, keeping them healthy all winter.

❄ Agave americana + 'Variegata'

The Century Plant

A beautifully shaped plant that makes its presence loud and clear in the garden. Large, weighty leaves curve gently outward forming an enormous tulip shape. They are blue-gray, have the appearance of being lightly dusted with white powder, and are edged with painfully sharp spines. Each leaf ends in a long sharp needle. The central core of the plant from which each new leaf unfurls is a solid mass, which remains unforgivingly rigid and capable of inflicting a savage wound. Growth is very slow. In fact, each leaf takes such a long time to emerge that the shape of the teeth from the leaf next in line remains as a permanent imprint. Over a period of thirty years, *A. americana* could reach dimensions of 5ft x 5ft (1.5m x 1.5m) if it is grown in a suitable site. Flower spikes are extremely impressive but are unlikely to be seen on plants less than twenty-five years old; some take as long as forty years or more, but rarely as long as the 100 years that its common name suggests.

Agaves make excellent choices for growing in pots. Plants become much hardier once they reach 2ft (60cm) and will also cope with cold winters more successfully if kept dry. Good drainage is vital and the soil should be very gritty so that any excess water can run away from the roots. Planting on a sloping site helps with the drainage even more, as any rain can easily drain away, instead of collecting in the central core of the plant. Keep fairly dry during the winter months.

After flowering the whole plant then dies. The variegated form of this plant is often available, but it is much less hardy than the type.

soil	Gritty and very sharply drained. Good for growing in pots or containers	
site	Full sun—brilliant for exposed or sloping gardens	
watering	Water regularly from late spring to early fall. Keep fairly dry during the winter	
general care	Feed annually in spring with blood, fish, and bone. Do not get any on the leaves, as they could become scorched	
pests & diseases	Watch out for slugs. Roots and leaves will rot in wet conditions. Mealy bug can be a problem on plants indoors	

Agave americana

Agave americana 'Variegata'

❄ *tender*

❄ Agave parryi

A pretty Agave with very neatly arranged chunky foliage that forms a clump shaped like an artichoke. Leaves are blue-gray and tipped with sharp spines. The whole plant rarely exceeds 18in (45cm) across and it can take twenty years to achieve these dimensions. This is the hardiest member of the whole Agave family, being capable of surviving many degrees of frost. However, this hardiness depends on how dry the conditions are during the winter which, for many climates, is an unlikely occurrence. Cold and dry weather is fine—cold and wet weather will turn the whole plant to a soggy mess very quickly indeed. For this reason, it is perhaps best to grow *A. parryi* in a large pot that can be brought under the cover of a porch or carport for the winter. This plant is named after Dr. Parry, who was the first person to collect seeds and introduce it into cultivation.

There are several different named varieties of *Agave parryi*. Most look virtually the same when young, but mature plants vary in their overall roundness of shape. All of them are very desirable in their own way, but the gold medal would have to go to *A. p.* var. 'Truncata', which is breathtakingly wonderful. Propagating these named varieties has to be done by offsets to ensure the production of identical offspring.

Although these plants are rarely seen growing in groups in their native regions of Arizona and Mexico, they look most fetching and quite natural if planted this way in desert gardens. The pronunciation of "Agave" seems to cause problems for some gardeners; the word, derived from the true Spanish name, is correctly pronounced "Ag-ah-vay," with the emphasis on the second syllable.

soil	Likes sharply drained soil with masses of added grit. Alkaline, neutral, or acid soil
site	Full sun—best grown in a large pot unless the garden is very mild
watering	Water regularly during growing season. Keep almost dry from mid-fall to early spring
general care	Give the plant a light application of food, such as blood, fish, and bone, annually in late spring
pests & diseases	Watch out for slugs. Roots and leaves will rot in wet conditions. Mealy bug can be a problem on indoor plants

Agave parryi

❄ Agave salmiana var. 'Ferox'

The most fearsome member of the *Agave* family and blessed with a suitably ferocious Latin name. This plant seems to have no common name, but "Vlad the Impaler" would be an appropriate suggestion. This vicious monster has large rigid leaves that are wide and flat, olive green in color, edged with sharp hooks and ending with an astonishingly dangerous tip several inches long—truly the stuff of nightmares and one of the most fantastic plants in the whole world. Dimensions of a fully grown plant can reach 4ft x 4ft (1.2m x 1.2m) and although not very hardy, except in the mildest gardens, it is perfect for a windy coastal garden or roof terrace as it is virtually hurricane-proof. It is a good choice for growing in a large pot which can be moved under the cover of a porch or put inside a frost-free shed during the winter. Although several degrees of frost can be tolerated, it is the wet and humidity during colder months that cannot be coped with. Larger plants are much hardier than small ones. Away from its native country of Mexico, it is unlikely to flower. Offsets are produced only occasionally. These should be removed from the parent plant and can be used for propagation or just thrown away.

soil	Any soil that is exceptionally gritty and free-draining is suitable for this plant
site	Full sun, best on a slope or bank to aid drainage. Copes with exposed conditions well
watering	Water regularly from late spring to early fall. Allow to almost dry out from mid-fall until mid-spring
general care	Feed annually in late spring with a mix of blood, fish, and bone, taking care not to get any on the leaves
pests & diseases	Mealy bug can be a problem. Roots and leaves can rot or suffer from fungal infections in cold, wet conditions

Agave salmiana var. 'Ferox'

❄ *tender*

❋ Aloe aristata
Torch Plant

Clump-forming succulent with individual stemless rosettes of around 8in (20cm) across. Foliage is dark green and streaked with white dotted lines (known as tubercles) across each leaf. The fleshy foliage contains a lovely slimy gel which can be used to soothe burns, just like its more famous cousin, *Aloe vera*. Despite originating from the Cape Province of South Africa, this plant is very hardy. In fact, it is the hardiest Aloe in existence. Flower stems rise out of the center of each rosette during the summer and last for many weeks. They are tall stems, which open out into orange-red elongated bells. *A. aristata* is slow-growing and it can take eight years for a clump to spread 3ft (1m).

Full sun is essential for them to flower. *A. aristata* can be used in rockeries, gravel gardens, containers, or planted out in any dry, sun-baked position. They look especially attractive planted in large, shallow, terracotta pots.

This succulent should be given a thorough soaking monthly from late spring through to early fall. At other times of the year, watering can be largely overlooked as long as *A. aristata* is planted outside. Indoors, keep the plant moist. It is easy to propagate from its offsets, which are produced in copious amounts.

Aloe aristata

Aloe aristata

soil	Thrives well in any soil that is gritty and sharply drained	
site	Full sun is essential if it is to flower. Grows well in large, shallow pots	
watering	Provide a thorough soaking monthly from late spring to early fall	
general care	Very little maintenance is necessary. A light feed once a year can be given if required	
pests & diseases	Rarely a problem if grown outside. Under glass, however, mealy bug is an occasional visitor	

❋ *hardy*

❄ Aloe striatula

An upright, branching succulent with long, pointed fleshy leaves that are full of thick syrupy jelly. Plants can easily reach 4ft (1.2m) tall with a spread of 3ft (1m) after five years. The flowers are stunning and usually produced in early summer. They are large and torch-shaped and are a loud bright yellow in color. These plants are hardy in most areas except really bad frost pockets. They perform particularly well in coastal gardens.

These plants need to be grown in the sunniest part of the garden and appreciate being against a warm wall, not only because this will make them flower more, but also because some support is needed to prop them up. They are so top heavy that if planted in a pot or in the middle of a border, they will topple over with the weight of the foliage. An annual feed is appreciated with something like a mix of blood, fish, and bone, sprinkled around the base in mid- or late spring. New plants need to be watered regularly throughout their first summer, but after that, watering can be more or less ignored.

Aloe striatula

Aloe striatula

soil	Any soil that is very well drained. Extra grit could be added for better drainage
site	Full sun in a sheltered spot, preferably against a wall for warmth and support
watering	New plants need watering but very drought-resistant once established
general care	Remove older brown leaves. After flowering, cut off old flower spikes as low down as possible
pests & diseases	Slugs adore these plants and can make unsightly scrapings along the surface of the leaves

❄ *hardy*

✳ Beschorneria yuccoides

Very similar in appearance to some types of yucca but without the spiky bits. It grows huge, clump-forming rosettes of glaucous green leaves, and batches of plants grown from seed can produce several forms, with noticeable variations in the width of the leaves. Very little seems to be known about *B. yuccoides* and it is quite rare in cultivation. However, despite its reputation for being only half-hardy, mature plants can shrug off many degrees of frost, certainly down to 19°F, providing the drainage is good.

The flower spikes are awesome. Massive coral-red stems 6ft (1.8m) long arch out of the center of the rosette, followed by numerous rose-red bracts, which in turn develop dozens of nodding green flowers, all of which last for many weeks, usually from late spring until mid-summer. They are quite a sight indeed. After flowering, large fig-like fruits appear. These are 2in (5cm) long and not edible. Individual rosettes die when they have flowered, but the plant as a whole carries on as normal, eventually forming more and more clumps.

Although any type of soil is acceptable, well-drained rich loam enriched with large dollops of rotted manure will help to get the very best from these plants. The quality of soil will determine the speed and size of growth—not just of the foliage, but the height and exuberance of the flower spikes, too.

When the flowers have finished and are starting to look a bit jaded, cut them off as low down into the foliage as possible. The rosette that has produced the flower will then slowly wither and die. This should be teased out of the plant when it has turned brown. Provided that the plant has been adequately fed and is growing well, lots more rosettes will be produced until sizeable clumps have been formed. On older plants, this means that several rosettes will reach maturity at the same time and several flower spikes across the plant will explode into growth at once, making a fine display.

Beschorneria yuccoides

Beschorneria yuccoides

	soil	Any well-drained soil is suitable, but rich and fertile conditions give the best results
	site	Full sun in a sheltered spot away from strong winds, which could cause damage
	watering	Once established, irrigation is not usually necessary unless grown in a pot
	general care	Annual feeding in the spring with a mix of blood, fish and bone will give excellent results
	pests & diseases	Slugs seem to enjoy the odd nibble. If grown in a conservatory, red spider mite can be a regular problem

✳ *hardy*

❄ Colletia cruciata

(syn. Colletia paradoxa)

An extremely unusual plant that has vicious leaves, which are actually modified branches, borne in pairs, and set at right angles to the ones directly beneath. They are flat, fleshy, and triangular with each one ending in a sharp tip. The flowers are a calm contrast to the foliage. They are dainty little bells of the very palest cream that waft the delicious scent of almonds around the garden for many months from the end of summer until early spring. Every butterfly for miles around is drawn to the blossom and, throughout the fall, *C. cruciata* is alive with numerous Red Admirals, Tortoiseshells, and Cabbage Whites. Bees also enjoy this plant immensely. This evergreen spiky plant is technically a small tree, although outside its native areas of Uruguay and Brazil, it is usually seen as a large bush—its width matching its height.

Full sun and very sharp drainage are essential requirements. Growth is fairly slow, so pruning should be necessary only if it starts to encroach where members of the family want to walk past. The whole plant is quite rigid and as the leaves are so brutal, they can easily tear holes in skin and clothing. It must be one of the most burglar-proof plants around. This is a plant that can be virtually ignored and

soil	Any soil type, preferably moderately fertile, as long as it is well drained
site	Full sun is ideal for this plant—excellent for exposed gardens
watering	If planted into the ground watering is rarely required, especially during winter
general care	Virtually maintenance-free but can thrive with an annual feed of a blood, fish, and bone mix
pests & diseases	Rarely a problem. This variety is refreshingly free from blight by pests and diseases

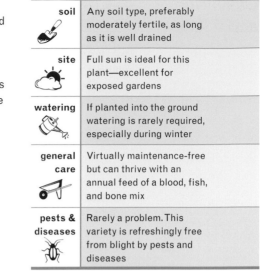

Colletia cruciata

Colletia cruciata

left to get on with life, but if given adequate growing space and a good helping of blood, fish, and bone annually, a height and spread of 8ft (2.5m) in ten years can be achieved. If forced to grow in a pot, it is very unhappy and can stay the same size for years, absolutely refusing to grow at all. For propagation purposes, semi-ripe cuttings planted into the soil is the best method to reproduce from this plant.

❄ *hardy*

❄ Dasylirion acrotrichum

This incredible plant has to be one of the best creations in the entire world. Mere words cannot do justice to *D. acrotrichum*. From the center of each rosette emerge hundreds of very thin, serrated leaves, all of which are tipped with a feathery tuft. As more and more leaves develop, the older ones are pushed down until a

soil	Any that is sharply drained. Extra grit in the planting hole would be beneficial
site	Full sun—excellent for planting on slopes or in exposed windy gardens
watering	Usually unnecessary unless grown in a pot, particularly during winter
general care	Sprinkle a couple of handfuls of blood, fish, and bone around the base of mature plants in late spring
pests & diseases	Relatively trouble-free. Pests and diseases do not usually cause any problems

beautiful arrangement begins to form, gradually building up into an almost perfect sphere. The overall size of a thirty-year-old plant can reach 5ft (1.5m) in diameter. After many years, as the older leaves are removed, a little stubby trunk starts to form. Absurd-looking flower spikes are occasionally sent out from the center, which can grow a few inches per day until they reach 3m (10ft). The flowers are pale yellow and might be classed as interesting rather than attractive. Spectacular as they are, they spoil the symmetry of the plant, which purists would find annoying. Simply chop them off as soon as they appear!

Dasylirions are the ultimate landscape plant as they can be appreciated from a distance. For this reason, they are best planted with plenty of space around them so that their amazing shape can be fully admired. They are practically hurricane-proof and can shrug off even the most severe salty gales, making them an excellent choice for the coast. Because they are so slow-growing, they are also suitable for planting in large terracotta containers.

Dasylirion acrotrichum

❄ *hardy*

Spiky & Succulent Plants

❄ Echeveria glauca

A delightful, clump-forming succulent that has fleshy leaves of the most beautiful shade of pale blue. Leaves interweave like those of a cabbage, making up individual rosettes of 6in (15cm) across. Because of their striking color, they have always been a popular addition to summer bedding schemes, especially those in gardens at coastal resorts. But in mild gardens, they can stay outside all year to become part of a permanent exotic planting plan. They are excellent in gravel gardens and superb choices for terracotta pots, where they can remain for many years due to their slow speed of growth. They could also be used to liven up rockeries. If planted in borders, they look much more effective planted in large groups, rather than just as single specimens. During the summer, each rosette can send up a 1ft (30cm) tall flower spike. Each stem contains several little bell-shaped flowers of bright red with yellow tips.

E. glauca hates to get its roots and lower leaves too wet, as they can easily rot away. For this reason, planting it on a sloping site will help any excess water drain away immediately.

Whether planted in the ground or in pots, top-dress the soil with gravel chips or colored grit. This not only shows off the plant's lovely color, but will also stop the rain from splashing any mud onto the leaves and spoiling their appearance. Apart from removing any old leaves or flower stems that have become brown and crispy, this plant will more or less take care of itself.

Propagation is easiest by division. However, leaf cuttings can also be used, but this is a much slower method of producing a good-sized plant. Propagating from seed is another possibility, but due to frequent hybridization of *E. glauca*, plants of varying quality and size will result.

Echeveria glauca

soil	Any soil that has lots of extra grit added to it will be suitable
site	Enjoys full sun—copes very well in exposed coastal gardens
watering	Water sparingly during the summer. Irrigation is unnecessary in the winter
general care	Apart from removing any old leaves or flower stems, this plant takes care of itself. Even feeding is unnecessary
pests & diseases	Slugs can ruin the look of the leaf surfaces. If grown in a pot, vine weevil will be the main enemy

❄ *tender*

❆ Puya chilensis

One of the hardiest members of the pineapple family, with a cleverly designed arrangement of leaves. They form a typical-looking rosette of foliage, with long strap-like leaves curving outward. The clever bit is how each leaf is edged with fearsome curved barbs all the way along both sides. These barbs enable the plant to trap passing small wildlife, which eventually rot down and provide nourishment for the plant (just try putting your hand in among the leaves to retrieve something...). But, as *Puya chilensis* is not generally hardy enough to grow outside year-round, and is best grown in a pot, this method of trapping is rarely put to the test in gardens outside its native Chile. If kept dry during the winter, several degrees of frost can be coped with. Apart from excess cold, the only way of killing this plant is by overwatering.

This is one of those rare plants that can happily spend all its life confined to a pot. It grows steadily to the size of the container and then stops. It can stay like this for years then, when it is eventually repotted, grows some more until it fills that one. In

cooler climates, flowering is quite rare, but the flower spikes are spectacular when they occur, even though the plant dies afterward. The stems are nearly 3ft (1m) tall and open out into greenish-yellow flowers that have a metallic look to them. They can last for many weeks.

soil	Well-drained gritty loam if grown in a pot. Outside, any well-drained soil
site	Full sun—tolerant of exposed positions. Keep dry in winter (bring under cover)
watering	Water occasionally just to stop the plant from drying out. Too much water can kill
general care	Remove any older brown leaves. Apply a light feed with a mix of blood, fish, and bone annually
pests & diseases	Rarely a problem. This variety is generally free from blight by pests and diseases

Puya chilensis

❄ Sempervivum spp.

Houseleek

There are probably hundreds of differently named Sempervivum varieties to choose from. They all look good if planted in large groups underneath taller spiky plants such as yuccas. But the best ones are the bigger, bolder varieties that are instantly more noticeable. Some of these such as 'Lady Kelly,' 'Commander Hay', or 'Old Lace' can have individual rosettes of up to 8in (20cm) across. None of them grows taller than 6in (15cm) and all of them are clump-forming. They come in a range of colors, mostly different shades of red or green. They send up little flower spikes during the summer, all of which are tipped with clusters of insignificant blooms that are usually pale pink, pale yellow, or white. Each individual rosette dies after flowering, but more plants are produced in great profusion to take their place.

Extra sharp drainage is essential for their well-being. They can cope with so little water that they can even be successfully

Sempervivum spp.

grown on the top of roofs, their roots being totally reliant on any rainwater that rushes down toward the gutters. They are also excellent choices for pots, troughs, and rock gardens where the soil is unlikely to be changed for years at a time, giving them the poor conditions that they seem to thrive in.

Because there are so many different kinds of Sempervivum to choose from, they are a plant that some gardeners love to have as collections, amassing as many different varieties as possible. However, they are most effective in large blocks of the same type.

Sempervivum spp.

soil	Poor, exceptionally well-drained soil, preferably with added grit
site	Full sun—excellent for exposed coastal positions, growing on slopes or banks
watering	Very little required. These plants do not appreciate wet winters
general care	Remove offsets when they have turned brown after flowering. Feed larger varieties annually
pests & diseases	Relatively trouble-free. Pests and diseases do not usually cause any problems

❄ *very hardy*

❋ Yucca aloifolia + 'Variegata'

Spanish Bayonet

A seriously architectural plant, being the most beautiful—and the most dangerous— yucca of them all. Each plant can be made up of several trunks topped with rosettes of long, shiny leaves. The relentlessly sharp spines at the end of each leaf show no remorse! The experience of walking into one of these will stay in the memory for some time.

Although slow-growing, each trunk could eventually grow to 7ft (2m). The total height including the head of foliage could be 10ft (3m) after twenty years. The dark green leaves cope with cold temperatures admirably—what they refuse to tolerate, however, is very cold weather combined with lots of rain. This combination will cause rotting and various fungal diseases. With this in mind, they either need a mild garden to grow in or to be planted in the shelter of a brick wall, or else they can be left in containers so that they can be moved to a drier place in the winter. Their slow speed of growth makes them suitable candidates for terracotta pots, provided that they are repotted every few years into something larger, otherwise they can become top-heavy

Yucca aloifolia 'Variegata'

soil	Exceptionally well-drained gritty soil is essential, but unfussy about the soil type
site	Full sun preferred, although the green version will cope with some shade
watering	If planted outside, hardly any water needed. In a pot, water regularly during the summer
general care	Yuccas need regular brown-bitting (see pages 22–23). Feed annually with blood, fish, and bone in early summer
pests & diseases	Generally trouble-free, as long as drainage is good. Black aphid can be a nuisance on the flower spikes

and fall over in strong winds. Whether grown in a container or in the ground, this plant is generally maintenance-free.

Short, stubby flower spikes open up into creamy white flowers tinged with purple at the base. They are waxy in texture and edible. They make a crunchy addition to salads although the taste is rather bland. A stunning variegated version is often available (see left), which has bright yellow edges to each leaf. It is less hardy than the straight green form. It is also smaller and even more slow-growing. If propagating, the green version of *Y. aloifolia* is easily produced from seed. The variegated version, however, must be grown from offsets produced by the plant.

❋ *hardy*

❄ Yucca glauca
Soapweed

One of the smaller yuccas, best grown close together in groups for full effect. The slender, straight, blue-gray leaves are edged with a narrow white stripe plus the occasional white fiber. The leaves are produced in such large numbers that the overall shape is almost a complete sphere. Each leaf is tipped with a small spine that looks harmless enough, but is still capable of inflicting a painful wound. After many years, a short trunk develops. Flower spikes over 3ft (1m) tall appear in the summer, producing dozens of individual flowers. They are creamy white, tinged with a dark pinkish-red, and contrast beautifully with the foliage.

Y. glauca is a very hardy species. The roots contain saponins, which lather up into a perfectly good soap, hence its common name. It is sometimes sold under its other name of *Y. angustifolia*. This yucca should always be planted directly into the ground—it never reaches its full potential if left in a pot.

Yucca leaf spot (Coniothyrium concentricum) can sometimes be a problem with this plant. This shows up as chocolate brown spots on the leaves. Affected leaves should be removed and burnt immediately, as this has a tendency to spread quickly to the rest of the plant.

soil	Exceptionally well-drained gritty soil is essential, but unfussy about the soil type
site	Full sun. Good in exposed positions and grown together in clumps
watering	Rarely needs to be watered once established, especially during winter
general care	Brown-bitting as required (see pages 22–23). Feed a mix of blood, fish, and bone around the base annually
pests & diseases	Yucca leaf spot can be a problem. Black aphid is a regular visitor to the flower spikes

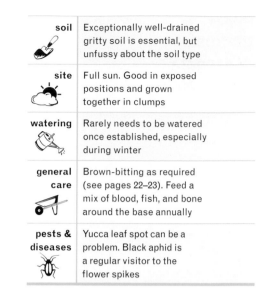

Yucca glauca

Yucca glauca

❄ *very hardy*

Yucca gloriosa + 'Variegata'

Spanish Dagger

Much loved by Victorian gardeners, *Y. gloriosa* slipped out of fashion with the introduction of flowery herbaceous borders, but it is an essential architectural requirement to any exotic garden. It has a strong evergreen shape that can add structure to any garden, a fact recognized by the famous Gertrude Jekyll, who used them in virtually all her planting schemes.

Y. gloriosa has big, bold rosettes of wide, stiff leaves, each one ending in a sharp point. It is very tough and will grow almost anywhere, even right on the coast where it can stand up to the fiercest salty gales. The flowers are spectacular. The thick red-tipped flower stalk pokes up out of the center of each rosette during late summer. Growing rapidly, it can easily reach 5ft (1.5m) before opening out into hundreds of large, waxy blooms. They are pale cream, tinged purple along the outer edges, very noticeable and much admired.

Y. gloriosa 'Variegata' is often available and just as hardy as its green counterpart. The leaves have bright yellow edges, making a welcome splash of color to a spiky border. It is unlikely to exceed 5ft (1.5m) in height. Old flower spikes should be removed, cutting down as low into the plant as possible. This will leave a flat area to begin with, but new growth will eventually form two or three branches from this point. Both the green and variegated versions can be planted singly or in groups; they can be planted to make an unusual hedge, they behave brilliantly in terracotta pots and, if planted underneath a window, can make a wonderful anti-burglar device. Brown-bitting of older leaves should be done when necessary (see pages 22–23).

Yucca gloriosa 'Variegata'

Yucca gloriosa

soil	Rich, well-drained loamy soil is best, but generally unfussy about the soil type
site	This plant is just as happy growing in full sun as it is in light shade
watering	Water regularly when first planted. After first season, usually takes care of itself
general care	Feed generously with blood, fish, and bone in early summer. Brown-bit older leaves (see pages 22–23)
pests & diseases	Watch out for black aphids on the flowers. In very wet winters, yucca leaf spot could be a problem

very hardy

Other Leafy Exotics

This chapter features a wide range of plants that includes perennials, herbaceous plants, wall shrubs, and plants that can be used for ground cover. These are often the most outrageous of architectural plants, grown not just for their amazing foliage, but also for their loud colorful flowers, such as the bananas, echiums, cannas, and ginger lilies. This group of plants also covers those with large, strongly shaped foliage such as fatsias, tetrapanax, melianthus, and mahonias.

Each of these plants in some way adds something special to an exotic and architectural garden, whether it has a jungly or Mediterranean theme. They all look good enough to be planted on their own or together with all of the other types of plants mentioned.

All have their own individual care requirements, but there are a few general rules that may help to keep them brimming with health and vigor. Plants with large, dark green leaves such as fatsias and mahonias generally prefer shade, while small-leafed plants with gray or succulent foliage such as corokia and lampranthus prefer a sunnier spot. Fast-growing plants with enormous leaves such as cannas and bananas must have masses of water, while plants that are slow-growing with tiny leaves such as rosemary and ephedra can usually adapt to drought conditions.

Unless your garden is huge, deciding what specimens to choose can be difficult as all of them are highly desirable.

❄ Acanthus mollis

Bear's Breeches

Enormous clumps of foliage are made up of huge, soft leaves 2ft (60cm) long and 1ft (30cm) across. Leaves are always glossy, as if they have just experienced a fresh shower of rain. The word "*mollis*" is a lovely choice for this plant—it means soft or velvety in Latin, describing the leaves perfectly. Flower spikes are very stately, towering above the foliage in large numbers during mid-summer. They have the appearance of large, pink and white lupins and can reach up to 5ft (1.5m) in height. The flower spike is made up of flowers and bracts, which are long-lasting. They make good cut flowers for indoors and are also suitable candidates for drying. Although classed by some as herbaceous, the classic behavior of dying down each winter occurs only in very cold gardens.

soil		Although this plant can grow in any soil, rich loam is preferred
site		Sun or light shade. Keep sheltered from wind as this tears the large leaves easily
watering		For best results, keep soil moist, particularly in growing season
general care		Annual feeding each spring is important. Remove any older yellow leaves, cutting right back to the base
pests & diseases		*Acanthus mollis* is a haven for slugs. Every slug in the entire neighborhood will find its way to this plant

Acanthus mollis

In a temperate climate, it remains beautifully green all through the year, making it an extremely architectural addition to any planting scheme.

Consider the planting position carefully. *A. mollis* detests root disturbance and will not usually survive being dug up and moved elsewhere. After a harsh winter, the foliage can take on a very tired appearance. If this happens, cut down all the leaves to the base. They will quickly re-shoot and provide masses of fresh new growth for the forthcoming season.

Acanthus mollis

❄ *very hardy*

❄ Agapanthus africanus
African Lily

Although the large clumps of leathery strap-like leaves are attractive in their own right, it is for the enormous flower spikes that this plant is usually grown. They are huge, towering up to 5ft (1.5m) above the foliage and opening up into large balls 1ft (30cm) across, balanced on the top of each stem. Each flower head is comprised of dozens of individual blossoms in either pure white or bright blue. They are stunningly gorgeous.

There are many other types of Agapanthus in cultivation that are much hardier than *A. africanus*, however it is worth forgoing the hardiness in exchange for the

Agapanthus africanus

Agapanthus africanus

soil	Rich, well-drained soil. Use soil-based potting mix with extra grit if planting in a pot
site	This plant appreciates full sun or light shade out of strong winds
watering	Water regularly during the growing season. Allow to dry out during the winter
general care	Feed from spring onward with regular doses of tomato food. After flowering, cut back stems as low as you can
pests & diseases	Generally trouble-free from pests and diseases, apart from the occasional rogue slug

size and shape of this plant's blooms, which are far superior to any of the others.

This plant is an unusual example of one that does better in a pot than it would if planted in the ground. The reason being is that if grown in a container, it is easy to move under cover if the weather becomes too wet and cold. Even in mild areas, these plants have been known not to reappear in the spring after a very soggy winter. The plants sulk and then rot away. Regular feeding with tomato food will produce the potash needed to persuade the plant to put its energy into producing flowers. After flowering, cut back the stems as low as you can.

❄ *tender*

❄ Aspidistra elatior
Cast-iron Plant

A. elatior is a familiar sight as a houseplant, but much less well known as a garden plant. However, in mild coastal gardens and sheltered cities, this plant will happily live outside. The dark, vegetable-like, evergreen leaves are joyously happy in temperatures down to 25°F. In colder winters, the leaves will bleach from the frost, but the roots will remain hardy and resprout the following spring. Maximum height is usually no more than 3ft (1m). This plant is incredibly slow to bulk up and it will take years to form a good-sized clump. Sometimes flowers appear at ground level. They are well tucked away among the foliage and not always noticed. They look like waxy primroses with pale lemon centers and dusky pink edges. Pollination of the flowers used to be attributed to slugs rummaging around at ground level, but this is now known not to be true. The common name refers to its robust nature and its ability to thrive on neglect. It was introduced from the Himalayas in 1822 and is native to both China and Japan. During Victorian times it was probably the most popular choice of plant available. It was the perfect houseplant for dark, smoky parlors where it could live happily for years. *A. elatior* is an excellent choice of plant for growing in a container due to its slow speed of growth.

Propagation of *A. elatior* is easily done by division, which is best undertaken in late spring or early summer. This plant is sometimes listed under the name of *Aspidistra punctata*.

soil	Will tolerate anything, but rich, free-draining soil will give the best results
site	Full shade, the deeper the better to keep the foliage a good strong color
watering	Appreciates adequate moisture, although it can survive quite well if ignored
general care	If cold weather bleaches the foliage, cut it down to ground level. Leaves will regrow the following year
pests & diseases	Outside, slugs could be a problem. Indoors, it can be troubled by red spider mite and scale insects

Aspidistra elatior

 tender

Other Leafy Exotics

✳ Astelia chathamica
Silver Spear

This plant has the most remarkable coloring of silver on each leaf, giving it the appearance of having been sprayed with metallic paint. Each sword-shaped leaf gently curves outward and can reach a length of 5ft (1.5m). Large, densely packed clumps can fill four square feet (1m x 1m) within five years of planting out if conditions are right. Flowers are disappointingly dull after the spectacular flamboyance of the silver leaves. They are bunches of yellow, bristly things that sprout out of the center of the plant and poke through the foliage in an apologetic manner. The stem and flower spike are about 1ft (30cm) in total and add nothing to the plant's appearance. They are therefore best removed as soon as they form.

The fact that these plants can grow as epiphytes living on trees gives some obvious clues as to how to grow *A. chathamica*. They thrive on neglect and are quite happy in pots that are infrequently watered. They are, however, best grown in the ground in a shady spot. Once planted, leave them alone—they manage quite well without constant fussing. Feeding is unnecessary, so is watering, except in periods of severe drought. Overwatering will cause the whole clump to rot very speedily. Check that any plants offered for sale are firm in their pots. If they rock around, they have been overwatered. They rarely recover, so leave them where they are.

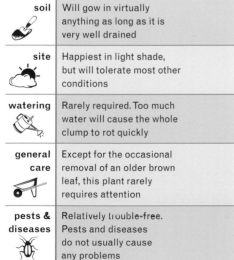

soil	Will gow in virtually anything as long as it is very well drained
site	Happiest in light shade, but will tolerate most other conditions
watering	Rarely required. Too much water will cause the whole clump to rot quickly
general care	Except for the occasional removal of an older brown leaf, this plant rarely requires attention
pests & diseases	Relatively trouble-free. Pests and diseases do not usually cause any problems

Astelia chathamica

✳ *hardy*

❄ Azorina vidalii

A low-growing, shrubby perennial with lots of long glossy leaves. Flower spikes appear during the summer, opening up into large, waxy bells of the palest china pink. They have a delicate appearance but, unfortunately, not a delicate fragrance to match. In fact, they have the aroma of unwashed socks about them. They last for weeks and weeks.

Although this plant is not very hardy, unless planted in a sheltered city or mild coastal garden, the fact that it is evergreen and slow-growing makes it an ideal choice for a pot. Therefore, in colder areas, it can live outside during the summer and be brought inside for the chillier months. Even a mature plant is unlikely to grow larger than 2ft x 2ft (60cm x 60cm). It is sometimes sold under its older name of *Campanula vidalii*.

soil	Any soil would be suitable, as long as it is free-draining. Too much water can be fatal
site	Happy in full sun or partial shade in a spot sheltered from cold winds
watering	Regular irrigation required during growing season; little watering during the winter
general care	Annual feed of blood, fish, and bone in spring. Flower spikes should be cut as low as possible after flowering
pests & diseases	Green aphids like the new shoots. During the winter, poor ventilation can cause botrytis (gray, fluffy mold)

A

Other Leafy Exotics

Azorina vidalii

❄ *tender*

❄ Baccharis patagonica
Magellan's Daisy Bush

This little evergreen shrub is an ideal choice for even the most hostile climate. Being buffeted by howling, icy, salt-laden gales is something that this incredibly tough plant takes in its stride back in its native homeland of southern Chile. *B. patagonica* is a thick mass of tiny, glossy leaves that grow slowly into a low mound of no more than 5ft (1.5m) tall and wide. Copious amounts of small, pale lemon daisies are produced in the summer, which give off a curious smell, reminiscent of freshly baked cakes. This lovely fragrance drifts around the whole garden, many feet from where the plant is growing. The name of *Baccharis* is thought to have derived from Bacchus, the God of Wine, with reference to the spicy aroma of the roots, which were sometimes added during winemaking. Its hardiness is foolproof, its only drawback is that it can be fairly short-lived. Propagation can be done from cuttings at almost any time of year.

soil	Will grow anywhere, in any soil type, except in very boggy ground
site	Happy in any spot, but a sunny open position gives the best results
watering	Prefers to be kept moist, but does not mind drying out occasionally
general care	Feeding unnecessary. Light pruning during late spring. However, do not cut too far back into the old wood
pests & diseases	Generally free from pests and diseases—a few aphids may cause a bit of grief during a hot summer

Baccharis patagonica

Baccharis patagonica

❄ *very hardy*

❄ Billbergia nutans
Queen's Tears

An exotic-looking plant, related to the pineapple and having shiny, strap-like leaves surrounding an urn-shaped center—a clever structure designed to catch every drop of available rainwater. The poor thing never expected that it might live out its days in rain-sodden climates, where its water-catching techniques are largely redundant. The flowers are very tropical-looking. Flamingo pink spears emerge from between the foliage and open out into pretty pink and green blossoms, which nod gently in the breeze. (The word "*nutans*" is Latin for nodding.) It is a clump-forming plant, which can spread to nearly 3–4ft (1m) across. Although commonly grown as a houseplant, it can thrive in temperatures down to 23°F.

soil	Any free-draining soil—can even be grown hanging off trees or other large plants
site	Will grow anywhere, but for the best results, grow it in light shade
watering	Frequent moisture gives the best results. Spray with water weekly if grown indoors
general care	Generally maintenance-free, once the correct position for the plant has been found
pests & diseases	Relatively trouble-free. Pests and diseases do not usually cause any problems

Billbergia nutans

Choosing the correct site for *B. nutans* can be tricky. In shady, moist positions, the foliage turns a lush deep green making for a much more attractive plant, but very few flowers are produced. In full sun, the foliage turns a yellowish-green, but the flowers are produced in abundance. A happy medium somewhere between the two would seem best. The soil must be free-draining, but frequent moisture is required. These plants can grow quite happily as epiphytes hanging off trees. Either wedge them between branches or place them on a bed of moss and tie them onto the trunk. For a real piece of tropical exotica, stuff them into the hairy stems of the hardy palm, *Trachycarpus fortunei*. They thrive in this sort of position and when established, can actually start to climb further up into the tree.

Other Leafy Exotics

B

❄ *tender*

❄ Canna indica
Indian Shot Plant

A splendid leafy addition to exotic planting schemes, having large, banana-type leaves and bright yellow and red flowers in summer. The name of "Indian shot plant" refers to the red that is splattered across the flowers. *C. indica* is one of the hardiest Canna lilies there are. It is an herbaceous plant, dying back to the rootstock each winter. It is fast growing and 5ft (1.5m) of new growth can be produced every year. Plants become bulkier as they age, eventually forming substantial clumps around 3–4ft (1m) across.

As *C. indica* puts on a serious amount of growth in one season, give it the best start by providing very rich soil and applying copious amounts of water from late spring until early fall. A foliar feed given with each watering will give an extra boost. Full sun is preferred but light shade gives good results, too. Canna lilies are traditionally used along seafronts in summer bedding displays. Their large leaves seem to cope well with the sea breezes and salty gales. By the time that really severe winter storms start, these plants will have died back.

soil	The best type of soil is one that is rich, moist and fertile
site	Prefers full sun, but also gives good results if grown in light shade
watering	Water a lot during the growing season, allow to dry out during the winter
general care	Add well-rotted manure in late spring at the start of the growing season. Cut back old leaves
pests & diseases	The tender juicy leaves are a magnet for every slug in the vicinity, so protection from them is vital

Canna indica

In milder areas, these plants can be left outside all year. In cold, wet areas, they are best dug up every winter and stored in dry peat in a greenhouse, in the same way that dahlias are treated. Alternatively, grow them in large pots, which can be moved under the shelter of a carport or inside a cool shed for the winter months. Another option is to leave them in their planting positions outside, and mulch heavily with straw or bracken when the foliage has been blackened by the frost and chopped back to the base with pruners.

Canna indica

❄ *tender*

❄ Canna iridiflora

Giant Canna Lily

A huge mass of giant leaves topped with the most outrageous, shocking-pink flowers. *C. iridiflora* can easily reach 8ft (2.5m) in a season before dying back each year, to reemerge the following spring with even more vigor than before. Although not very hardy, it can just about cope with temperatures down to 25°F. This plant is one of the most essential plants for any garden with exotic tendencies. Because of their size, they perform less well in windy positions than other varieties of Canna.

Fertile soil, enriched with well-rotted manure, is necessary to get the best from these leafy subjects. They must never be deprived of water during the entire growing season. A sunny spot is preferred, but light shade is acceptable. After the first frosts, their leaves will be scorched and the foliage should then be cut back right to ground level. In mild gardens, clumps can be left in the ground and mulched with straw or bracken. In cold, wet gardens, they are best lifted out of the ground and stored in dry peat under a bench in a cold greenhouse, in much the same way as the more familiar dahlias. If plants produce large quantities of lush green leaves each year, but no flowers, introduce tomato food to their menu in early summer. This will provide the extra dose of potash required for flower production. These plants are best bought from nurseries that pride themselves on accurate labeling. Alternatively, make sure they are bought when flowering.

Canna iridiflora

Canna iridiflora

soil	The favored soil for this plant is one that is rich, moist, and fertile
site	Enjoys sun or light shade, but must be in a sheltered spot
watering	Copious amounts during the growing season, allow to dry out during the winter
general care	Add well-rotted manure in late spring at the start of the growing season. Cut back old leaves when frosted
pests & diseases	Slugs congregate from all around to feast on the appetizing foliage, so protect against them

❄ *tender*

Carpobrotus edulis

Hottentot Fig

Fast-growing succulent ground cover that can spread over enormous distances, given the right spot. In mild coastal areas, it can often be seen cascading down cliffs or scrambling along the edges of beaches. It is exceptionally salt-tolerant and is an essential requirement for any seaside garden. It copes with hostile, exposed positions so well that it could almost be considered as a type of aristocratic seaweed. The evergreen foliage is made up of thick chunks, strung together like sausages. In milder areas, large and often brightly colored daisy flowers open up during the day. They can be white, magenta, vivid pink, pale pink, red, or yellow. In hot summers, these are followed by luscious edible fruits that are sweet and sticky. In cold winters, the leaves may be cut back hard by severe frost, but it always regrows with a vengeance the following year.

This plant grows very badly in a pot. It usually ends up consisting of a few stringy bits dangling miserably down the sides. It is much better to buy them from nurseries, which grow them in deep seed trays—this gives *C. edulis* a better surface to cling to. It is sometimes sold under the name of *Mesembryanthemum edule*.

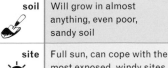

soil	Will grow in almost anything, even poor, sandy soil
site	Full sun, can cope with the most exposed, windy sites with ease
watering	In first season, give regular soakings. Once established, irrigation is unnecessary
general care	Although happy to survive on neglect, a light feed at the beginning of the season will give good results
pests & diseases	Not a problem. Nothing seems to bother this tough plant—it can't even be destroyed by fire!

Carpobrotus edulis

Carpobrotus edulis

❄ *tender*

Corokia x virgata

C. x virgata is a plant ignored disdainfully by some and adored by others, but this pretty shrub from New Zealand has so many virtues that it ought to be very widespread. Maybe it needs a glamorous common name—the New Zealand Olive, perhaps?

This is a naturally occurring hybrid between *C. cotoneaster* and *C. buddlejoides*, and consists of a mass of tiny leaves that are dark green with a metallic bronze sheen on the top surface and powdery white beneath. Very small, yellow daisy flowers appear during late spring and early summer on the previous year's growth. These are then followed by bright orange berries.

If the appearance alone doesn't convince anyone to rush out and buy it, perhaps its character might. This is one of the most salt-tolerant plants around, making it an excellent choice for a windy position or coastal garden. It can be left as a large, wild-looking shrub; it can be clipped tidily into a smaller, more shapely plant; or else it can be cut formally into a hedge. Its height is unlikely to exceed 8–10ft (2.5–3m) away from its native country and it will take many years to reach this size.

This is a very easy plant to cultivate. It can cope with many different conditions and a wide range of soils, including chalk. The only conditions it seems to dislike is very boggy ground. Poor soil is not a problem, although like many plants, much better results occur if the soil is fertile or enriched with well-rotted manure or a couple of handfuls of blood, fish, and bone in spring. A site in full sun gives a tighter and more compact mass of foliage, but light shade is acceptable, too. If a hedge is required or the plant lives in a pot, regular clipping will obviously be necessary.

soil	Will tolerate most types of soil, but grows best in fertile, well-drained conditions
site	Full sun preferred—good in gardens exposed to the wind and ocean
watering	Once established, takes care of itself; in a container, water during growing season
general care	Appreciates an annual feed each spring. Can be clipped into shape after flowering
pests & diseases	Relatively trouble-free. Pests and diseases do not usually cause any problems

Corokia x virgata

❄ *hardy*

Crocosmia 'Lucifer'

Montbretia

The fiery scarlet flowers are the main appeal of this plant. They are not just vividly colored but are also produced in copious amounts. They are long-lasting and a popular choice for flower arrangers, although they add such strong splashes of color to a garden, it is best to leave them on the plant to enjoy outdoors. They are grown from corms and die back each fall. Growth starts again during mid- to late spring, sending up lots of grassy leaves, which open out into narrow sword shapes. The foliage can be up to 3ft (1m) tall with the flower spikes adding another 2ft (60cm) on top of that.

This plant starts to flower in late summer and carries on through the fall when most other plants have stopped flowering for the year. Most Crocosmia plants have bright orange or vermilion flowers, but the variety 'Lucifer' has the loudest red of all—so bright that it is almost fluorescent. It is also the earliest variety to send up its long, wiry flower stems each year.

soil	Prefers to grow in light, moderately fertile soil that is free-draining
site	Full sun or light shade, ideally sheltered from strong winds
watering	Keep moist during the growing season, but the soil should never become boggy
general care	Feed in spring with well-rotted manure. In the fall after the foliage has turned brown, cut back hard to ground level
pests & diseases	Relatively trouble-free. Pests and diseases do not usually cause any problems

Crocosmia 'Lucifer'

Crocosmia 'Lucifer'

These plants are best grown in large drifts to give a dramatic effect. They bulk up quickly and can spread over fairly wide areas. A small woodland garden would be perfect where they can naturalize without having their *wanderlust* curbed. If they outgrow their allocated space in the garden, dig up chunks with a spade and dispose of them or replant elsewhere. They are hardy in most areas, but in exceptionally cold gardens, the bulbs are best lifted and stored for the winter in trays of fairly dry peat under a greenhouse bench.

※ *very hardy*

❄ Cynara cardunculus
Cardoon

A huge brute of a plant that grows with amazing speed after its winter dormancy, putting on new growth every day during mid- to late spring. The leaves are deeply cut, soft to the touch, pale greenish-gray in color and achieve enormous dimensions. An established plant that has been overwintered in the ground can easily grow 8ft (2.5m) high and over 6ft (2m) wide during the growing season. It looks just like a giant vegetable plant towering against the sky, which in one sense is just what it is. (In France, it is commonly grown for its edible stems, which are blanched like celery.) In most gardens, however, it is grown as an ornamental plant, perfect for the back of planting schemes. Rising above the foliage in mid- to late summer, flower stems become visible. The flower heads start off looking like mini artichokes, then open up into large thistles. These are actually electric blue but photographs (as you can see!) never do justice to this color so try and see some in the flesh.

Cynara cardunculus

After flowering, the leaves look good for several months, but in the winter, they start to turn a bit tired and yellow, and are best cut down to the ground. Within a short time, new buds start to form at the base of the old stalks and a small amount of growth is produced. With the start of the warmer weather, growth accelerates rapidly to begin the whole process again. New plants should be planted in late spring or early summer and left in the ground permanently.

soil	Must be put into very rich and fertile soil to achieve maximum growth
site	Full sun preferred in a sheltered spot, protected from strong winds
watering	Lots of water required during the growing season, but it must not become boggy
general care	Feed heavily in mid-spring with lots of well-rotted manure or several handfuls of blood, fish, and bone
pests & diseases	Adored by slugs and snails, which leave slime trails and large holes all over leaves if not dealt with rapidly

Cynara cardunculus

❄ Danae racemosa

Alexandrian Laurel

D. racemosa is often classed as just an evergreen shrub, which is rather unkind as this oddity deserves a more interesting label. Describing this plant is not easy, as it is somewhere between a miniature bamboo and a bunch of asparagus. The new shoots are the start of its "asparagus" phase, poking up through the ground in mid- to late spring. These grow up to about 2–3ft (60–70cm) and open out into wiry stems with "leaves" along the length. Although they look like leaves and serve the same function as leaves, they are blessed with the delightful-sounding name of "cladode," which is horticultural-speak for a sort of flattened branch. Many shoots are sent out each spring which remain year-round. As the plant matures, larger clumps of it begin to form, hence its "bamboo" phase. *D. racemosa* is very slow to spread, and after ten years will probably extend to only 3ft (1m) or so. After a very warm summer, numerous bright red berries appear, usually during the early fall.

Apart from its desirable looks, this plant is extremely useful for places in the garden where little else will grow. Deep, dark shade can be tolerated and so can dry conditions, making *D. racemosa* especially valuable for growing beneath evergreen trees. Given a choice, however, light shade in moist soil would be the optimum growing site. This is a great favorite for flower arrangers, as it still looks fresh after several weeks in a vase.

The name of Danae refers to one of the daughters of the splendidly named King Acrisius of Argos. It is native to Iran and Asia Minor, and was introduced into cultivation in the 1700s. This plant is very closely related to the better-known Butcher's Broom (*Ruscus aculeatus*). Propagation is very easy, either from fresh seed or by division in early spring.

soil	Rich soil is preferred, but poorer conditions can be coped with quite easily
site	Light shade is best, but deep shade is also perfectly acceptable
watering	Although regular irrigation gives the best results, dry positions can be tolerated
general care	Generally maintenance-free. Old shoots can be cut back to ground level in the spring
pests & diseases	Rarely a problem if grown in the ground, but if confined to a pot, vine weevil are virtually guaranteed

Danae racemosa

❄ *very hardy*

❄ Daphne odora 'Aureomarginata'

A small, evergreen plant that grows into a beautiful blobby shape without the assistance of any clipping. The shiny foliage forms a rounded dome made up of fresh green leaves that are subtly edged with pale cream variegation. Flowers open up from mid-winter until early spring when there is very little else in flower in the rest of the garden, which makes them especially welcome. They are small, flattened clusters of rose pink blossoms, which give off the most heavenly perfume. If grown near a door or window, the fragrance can be appreciated each time they are opened, casting scent all around the room. This is one of the best possible choices for a chalky garden. The only slight drawback with *D. odora* 'Aureomarginata' is that it can be a bit short-lived, and may have to be replaced every few years.

It is rare to see a clump bigger than 4ft (1.2m) across. Unusually for a variegated plant, it is hardier and more robust than the straight green version. Choose the planting position carefully, as digging it up and replanting somewhere else would almost certainly lead to its death.

soil	Flourishes best in neutral to alkaline soil that is well drained
site	Full sun or light shade. Choose position carefully as replanting is likely to kill it
watering	Soil should be kept moist and not allowed to dry out or become too boggy
general care	Give a light feed with a handful of blood, fish, and bone in late spring. Other maintenance rarely required
pests & diseases	Green aphids are often seen feasting around the new growing tips of this plant

Daphne odora 'Aureomarginata'

❄ *very hardy*

❄ Echium pininana

E. pininana reigns supreme as King of all the exotics. If your garden is a mild one, this woody herb is unquestionably essential. Warm city gardens are ideal, but milder coastal gardens are best of all, as this plant really thrives in the salty sea air. They look spectacular planted in large groups for maximum effect, but if this is not possible due to lack of space, try to find room for a small gathering of at least five. They have a life cycle which spreads over two years, starting with the planting of small seedlings in early spring. These will grow fairly rapidly during their first growing season, forming leafy masses 4–5ft (1.5m) tall by the end of the summer. The stem will be quite thick and woody. Take care when handling them and always wear gloves—they are densely covered with bristles that rub off easily, causing an itchy rash if they manage to get under the skin. The leaves at this stage will be large and lush, with a distinctively tropical aura about them. Getting *E. pininana* through the first winter is the real challenge. They are difficult to wrap up and protect from frost, which is why they can only be grown successfully in warmer areas.

Assuming, they have come through the winter unscathed, this is where the fun bit starts. Growth starts early, usually in the early spring. With surprising rapidity, the stem starts to get longer and longer, and the new foliage becomes smaller and smaller as the stem extends and romps away into the air. By late spring, the stems can be towering 12ft (4m) into the air, and flower buds are starting to become more obvious. They cover the entire top half of the stem, which by now has reached its maximum height and tapered off at the top. The flowers are a truly wonderful sight. They open out into hundreds of purplish-blue blossoms, which are not only a joy to look at, but are sheer heaven to the local bees. Flowers last for many weeks but then, unfortunately, that is the end of the plant, which dies and has to be disposed of. One compensation, however, is that many seeds will probably be scattered all around the garden and will pop up in the most unexpected gaps such as paving and between other plants.

soil	Any, but a good quality, well-drained soil is preferred for best growth	
site	Full sun or light shade. Thrives in mild, coastal gardens	
watering	Required only when newly planted. Otherwise takes care of itself	
general care	Once planted, leave them where they are as they hate root disturbance. Protect from frost during winter	
pests & diseases	Relatively trouble-free. Pests and diseases do not usually cause any problems	

Echium pininana

Echium pininana

❄ *tender*

✳ Ephedra spp.

Mormon's Tea

There are several species of this weird-looking plant, all so similar that even the most accomplished gardeners admit to having difficulty telling them apart. However, they are all evergreen and most are totally hardy. Thick, feathery, bright green masses creep along the ground or tumble over walls and banks, providing total cover. Slender, jointed stems with small, scale-like leaves give Ephedra the appearance of a conifer crossed with the common horsetail weed. Small, pale lemon catkins are produced during a hot summer, followed very rarely by red edible fruits. Ephedra are of great botanical interest rather than plants of great beauty, but once a mature clump that is growing well has been viewed, they are usually given greater respect. Large swathes can cover a considerable area.

This is a very easy plant to cultivate, although it is hopeless in a pot. To keep it looking good, plant in full sun in light, very well-drained soil, preferably on a sloping site, where excess rain can run away immediately. Virtually no maintenance or pruning will be required for this plant. Even weeding will be eliminated, because of the thick ground cover that this plant provides.

soil	Can tolerate any soil type, providing it is very sharply drained
site	Full sun is preferred, although some shade can be tolerated
watering	Required only for newly planted specimens—takes care of itself otherwise
general care	This plant requires practically no maintenance whatsoever or pruning of any kind
pests & diseases	Relatively trouble-free. Pests and diseases do not usually cause any problems

Ephedra is seen growing in many different countries, including parts of the United States, where a rather unpleasant beverage used to be made from its leaves by some early settlers, hence its common name. The plant has medicinal uses, too: a handy treatment for the relief of asthma can be derived from an alkaloid contained in some ephedras, namely ephedrine.

Ephedra

❄ Eryngium agavifolium

A spiny perennial plant that usually manages to stay evergreen through the winter, except in really cold areas. However, if the frost is severe enough to cut the foliage back to the ground, it always regenerates the following spring and takes only a few weeks to regain its previous form. Leaves are wide, look highly polished, and are a bright emerald green. They feel leathery to the touch and are edged with hooked barbs, which look more ferocious than they actually are. Away from their native country of Argentina, the ultimate height and spread is rarely more than 2ft (60cm). They grow in clumps from a stemless base. Flower spikes are sent up during early summer and look like large greenish-yellow thimbles on short stalks. They are not exactly things of ravishing beauty, and it is tempting to cut them off. But as bees, wasps, and flies flock around them in large numbers, it would be a pity to spoil their enjoyment.

E. agavifolium is very easy to cultivate and looks better planted in groups of at least three plants to make them more noticeable. They are ideal for the front of borders, or in rockeries, or planted in gravel gardens. They are not suitable for growing in pots as the roots are very vigorous and tend to dry out quickly unless the plant is watered frequently.

soil	Light, sandy, free-draining soil is best—grows well in rocky places
site	Full sun required. Hopeless in a pot—must be planted in the ground
watering	Water frequently until established—it will then take care of itself
general care	In a harsh winter, foliage can become shabby. The whole plant should be cut back to the ground with a sharp knife
pests & diseases	Slugs can be a nuisance so protect against them, and green aphids are fond of the new shoots

Eryngium agavifolium

❄ *very hardy*

❄ Euonymus fortunei 'Kewensis'

Slow-growing ground cover for those awkward places in the garden where it is difficult to know what to plant. It has a mass of dainty, prostrate stems that are edged with tiny leaves and can creep along the shadiest of places, providing an evergreen underblanket for trees and shrubs, as an alternative to a chipped bark mulch. To get total cover within three or four years, generous numbers must be planted, as one plant will spread no more than a couple of square feet (half a square meter) during this amount of time. This plant can also be persuaded to become a climber if it is pushed against a fence lined with trellis. It will need to be tied on manually, as it is very lazy about finding its own way up but, because of this reluctance to cling to any object that comes its way, it does not become a tangled mess and therefore makes tidy edging for stone walls or banks, and can even be allowed to dangle out of window boxes, provided that they are of a sufficiently large size.

E. fortunei 'Kewensis' will grow in most places, whether in sun or shade. Most soil types are acceptable but, to get the darkest green color, it is best grown in shade in moist, fertile, lime-free conditions. The leaves have a slightly glossy surface but, if deprived of water, can quickly lose their luster. For this reason, it is best not to try and grow it underneath plants that guzzle all the available moisture, such as bamboos. Euonymus is supposed to bring good fortune to whoever plants it, so if a run of bad luck has been experienced recently... well, maybe it's worth a try. This plant has probably evolved from E. fortunei radicans, as it looks exactly the same, but as 'Kewensis' is a much more dwarf version, it has been given its own name.

Euonymus fortunei 'Kewensis'

soil	Neutral to acid preferred. Best grown in fertile, lime-free soil
site	Shade is preferred but can also grow in full sun, preferably with some shelter
watering	Must be kept moist, especially if grown in full sunshine
general care	This specimen is generally maintenance-free, because of its use mainly as a ground cover plant,
pests & diseases	Relatively trouble-free. Pests and diseases do not usually cause any problems

❄ *very hardy*

Euphorbia mellifera

Honey Spurge

E. mellifera is, arguably, the finest member of the vast Euphorbia family. The foliage is similar to that of an Oleander, but a much nicer color. The leaves are of such a bright emerald green that they appear almost luminous and, as they are evergreen, they are particularly pleasing on a dreary winter's day. This plant grows into a neat, dense domed shape of over 7ft (2m) high and the same width. It is fast-growing and can reach this size within three years. The common name of "Honey Spurge" refers to the flowers, which are not only honey-colored but have the same delicious smell, too. They appear in liberal quantities during late spring.

Euphorbia mellifera

soil	*Euphorbia mellifera* prefers a rich and fertile soil type
site	Sun or light shade in a sheltered spot—the warmest site possible
watering	Water well to start with—once established, it can take care of itself
general care	Can be clipped back if it gets too big, even back to the base if it becomes too "leggy"
pests & diseases	Check for capsid bug and aphids. If grown under glass, whitefly and red spider mite are troublesome

The flattened clusters of flowers give off their wonderful aroma when fully open on a warm day.

E. mellifera is hopeless in a pot, so plant it out into rich, fertile soil in a sunny or lightly shaded spot. It becomes very leggy if planted in deep shade, although this can be resolved if pruned back hard to the base every spring. Wear gloves when cutting into this plant, as the milky white sap that is exuded from the cut stems and leaves of all Euphorbias can be an irritant to eyes and skin. Avoid planting in windy or exposed sites and if the garden is a bit of a frost pocket, choose the warmest spot possible, preferably by the shelter of a sunny wall. In perfect conditions, specimens could eventually reach 10ft (3m) across. Feeding is not usually necessary except in very poor soils.

As for pests, if your garden is plagued with rabbits, this is one of their last choices, as the bitter sap makes for an unpalatable lunch.

Euphorbia mellifera

❄ *hardy*

❄ Euphorbia myrsinites

Myrtle Spurge

E. myrsinites is the perfect ground cover to complement all of the spiky plants such as Yuccas and Agaves. It adores full sun and drapes itself all around the base of every plant it encounters, providing a thick undercover. The long, fleshy runners are edged with blue leaves, which are small and attractively shaped into a point. They look succulent like those of a desert plant but, when inspected more closely, are in fact quite flat. The flowers (which are really protuberances called bracts) are bright greenish-yellow and appear during early spring. Inside each one is the true flower, which is a tiny yellow dot. One plant can cover an area of around two square feet (half a square meter) in two years.

This plant remains evergreen and is totally hardy. Older plants can eventually become a bit straggly, but this can be solved by pruning them back fairly hard, which encourages new growth to sprout from the central rosette. Wear gloves when cutting into Euphorbias, as the milky sap that pours from the cut stems and leaves can be irritating to the skin. Full sun is an essential requirement so that the growth remains as bushy as possible. Poor soil is quite acceptable and good drainage is vital. Too much water collecting around the roots is a guaranteed way of killing the whole plant very quickly. This plant is an easy one to cultivate—even annual feeding can be dispensed with.

soil		Grows in any soil—even poor soil is acceptable as long as it is well drained
site		To get the best from this plant, full sun is an essential requirement
watering		Required when first planted, but after that, ignore except during long, dry periods
general care		After flowering, cut off the dead flower spikes back to the leafy parts of each stem
pests & diseases		Relatively trouble-free. Pests and diseases do not usually cause any problems

Euphorbia myrsinites

❄ *very hardy*

Euphorbia wulfenii

Spurge

Dramatic evergreen perennial that is easy to grow and totally hardy. This is a versatile plant that can be successfully incorporated into most planting schemes. It can look just as good with spiky plants as it does in a shrubby or flowery border. It looks rather fetching in gravel gardens where the color of the leaves can be shown off to good effect. In spacious gardens, *E. wulfenii* looks wonderful if planted in large groups. Foliage is a dark, steely blue and produced in abundance to make a very bushy plant that can reach 4ft (1.2m) tall and the same in width within five years. The showy flower heads are made up of startling sulfur yellow bracts, surrounding a tiny yellow dot, which is the real flower. They last for many weeks from early to late spring.

This plant is unfussy in its requirements, although it has several preferences, given the choice. A sunny spot will give the best results, but it seems quite content in light shade, too. Any soil will do, although it does have a penchant for chalky conditions. Good drainage is essential but the type of soil does not seem to matter much. Poor soil is totally acceptable, although rich fertile conditions get the plant off to a much quicker start. This plant does especially well in coastal gardens, where salty winds do not seem to be a problem. The only place it hates to be is in a small pot, where root restriction will turn it into a hideous leggy-looking object fairly rapidly.

Propagation is easy from seed—buy this from a reputable seed company instead of collecting it yourself. These plants hybridize easily and can produce very variable adult plants. As with all Euphorbias, take care of the milky sap which oozes from the stem when it is cut. This can be an irritant to both skin and eyes.

Euphorbia wulfenii

Euphorbia wulfenii

soil	Fertile soil is preferred, but will cope with poor chalky conditions
site	Full sun or light shade. Grows particularly well in coastal gardens
watering	Drought-tolerant once established. Soil must be well drained
general care	Remove old flower heads when they turn brown. If plant becomes too leggy, prune it back to the base
pests & diseases	Relatively trouble-free. Pests and diseases do not usually cause any problems

※ *very hardy*

✳ Fasciularia bicolor

Firewheel

This is the hardiest member of the family *Bromeliaceae*, which means it is closely related to the pineapple. It is made up of tightly packed bundles of narrow, prickly leaves. These mass together forming individual rosettes that pile up on each other, gradually creating huge clumps of impenetrable foliage. They either spread sideways across the ground or hang down over stone walls. If gently coaxed in the right direction, they can even be persuaded to climb up fibrous tree trunks. During the summer, the center of mature rosettes produces astonishing vivid scarlet inner leaves circling a center of bright turquoise blue flowers.

If grown correctly, this lovely exotic plant from Chile can cope with surprisingly low temperatures. Sharp drainage is the one essential requirement. If grown in the ground, a sloping site is preferred so that any excess water drains away. It is a perfect choice for planting in a stone trough, for hanging over walls, and growing on rockeries. It can even be tied into trees where it is

quite happy growing as an epiphyte. It is good fun to tie it onto the base of a hairy-trunked tree such as the hardy palm, *Trachycarpus fortunei*. As it grows, the roots cling to the fibrous matting and gradually haul themselves up into the tree where they can live for years hanging onto the entire length of the tree trunk.

soil	Free-draining gritty soil. If in a pot, use a soil-based potting mix with extra grit
site	Full sun or light shade—can also cope well in exposed conditions
watering	Water infrequently. Plant takes care of itself once established
general care	No maintenance required, except for cutting out the old rosettes if they become scruffy
pests & diseases	Rarely a problem, although the old dead flower heads can sometimes attract large numbers of woodlice

Fasciularia bicolor

❋ Fatsia japonica

Japanese Fatsia

As *F. japonica* is sometimes sold in stores as a houseplant, it is often assumed that this plant is not hardy enough for the garden. However, not only is it hardy, but it is so tough that it can be planted outside in virtually any climate. It is a fantastic addition to a jungly garden and can cope brilliantly with deep shade. The leaves are huge, lobed, and leathery. They have a glossy top surface and are deep green in color, provided that they are kept in the shade where they are happiest. If grown in a sunny spot, the foliage turns a horrid, sickly greenish-yellow and looks most unappealing.

Mature plants can easily reach 8ft (2.5m) tall and 7ft (2m) wide, so plenty of space must be left around it when planting. Growth is slow, so it makes a reasonably good choice for a large container, where it could live for several years before planting out into the garden. There is nothing delicate about this plant—it is large and heavy-looking with plenty of dense growth. It would be the perfect plant for filling a large and shady corner. In late summer, cream-colored flower spikes, a bit like drumsticks, rise up from the center. They are very unexciting and can be removed if they are unappreciated. If they are left on the

Fatsia japonica

soil	Although rich, fertile soil is preferred, this is a surprisingly unfussy plant
site	Thrives best in shade—if left in full sun, leaves become yellowish
watering	Plenty of moisture is required, especially if grown in a pot
general care	Feed heavily mid-spring with lots of blood, fish, and bone sprinkled around the base. Remove older, yellow leaves
pests & diseases	Black aphid is often found on new shoots; capsid bug can also spoil the large leaves, so check regularly

plant, bunches of tiny inedible black fruits appear when the flowers have finished.

If the plant becomes too tall, just chop through the stem at any height—new leaves will soon appear from the cut end. An alternative pruning idea is to remove all of the lower branches and retain only one single main stem with foliage on the top. That way it looks even more exotic, closely resembling a papaya. Pruning is not compulsory, however, and the whole plant can just be left to grow naturally. There is a variegated form available, with green and pale cream leaves. It is a fine-looking plant, but less hardy, slower growing, and much less chunky than the straight green version.

❋ *very hardy*

✳ Fremontodendron 'California Glory'

Flannel Bush

This plant is difficult to categorize, but is probably best described as a wall shrub. It is not self-clinging but enjoys resting against a sun-baked wall where it can spread out flat. It could reach 16ft (5m) in height within five years if growing well. The eventual width is usually around half of its height. It is almost evergreen, but tends to go a bit thin during the winter. Leaves are quite sparsely

Fremontodendron 'California Glory'

soil	Poor and well-drained. Especially good for chalky or sandy soils
site	Full sun, preferably by a sun-baked wall in the warmest part of the garden
watering	Water frequently until established—it then will become drought-tolerant
general care	No feeding required. Rarely needs pruning but if this becomes necessary, prune immediately after flowering
pests & diseases	Not usually prone to any ailments or particular pests—a fairly trouble-free plant to grow

produced and are mid-green in color and covered in a dusty powder. This dust is harmless to most people but occasionally it can cause an allergic reaction if it is inhaled. Some people (myself included!) cannot get close to it without experiencing a mild asthma attack. Although not desperately architectural or particularly noticeable in the winter, there is one excellent reason for having this plant in the garden—the flowers. They are wonderful, just like giant buttercups. They are loud yellow in color, are produced in copious amounts, and last for many weeks during early summer.

This plant is a bit of a fusspot and can take a while to get going. Choose the planting site carefully as, once planted, it resents any root disturbance so cannot be transplanted elsewhere. It can also be somewhat short-lived, but it is worth all the grief in exchange for those lovely blooms. The base of a sun-baked wall is not only a good place to plant it for the support that can be offered, but it is also likely to be one of the hottest places in the garden, with the sun reflecting off the bricks. These warm conditions will produce more flowers. The drier conditions that are likely to occur are also appreciated, as this plant becomes exceptionally drought-tolerant once established. Fremontodendron is sometimes listed as Fremontia, and the 'California Glory' variety is a cross between two species.

Fremontodendron 'California Glory'

❄ Gunnera manicata

Giant Rhubarb

Not a plant for the timid gardener. With almost no care at all, *G. manicata* can be big; with proper care and attention this plant can be an absolute monster. With both its size and its wonderful family name of *Haloragidaceae* added together, we have a plant that is pure fantasy. The leaves are enormous, reaching over 1½ft (half a meter) across, with a surface that is rough and crinkled. Hundreds of waxy barbs cover the stems and extend along the veins on the undersides of each leaf. The stems can get so large that it is possible to stand underneath them and look up into the leaves that form a canopy far above. The stems and leaves all grow from a central crown that gets bigger and bulkier each year. This is the delicate part of the plant and can need some protection during the winter, especially in its earlier years. As the leaves die back each year after the first frosts, it is both practical and traditional to fold the brown frosted foliage over the crown, so giving it some useful on-site protection. This can be left on all winter until growth starts again the following spring. The previous year's foliage

	soil	Is unfussy, but does prefer rich, moist, and fertile conditions
	site	Sun or shade in a sheltered spot. Shade draws the plant up, making leaves even larger
	watering	A regular supply of water will be required throughout the plant's life
	general care	Removing the flower spikes before they open will put all the plant's energy into making bigger leaves
	pests & diseases	Relatively trouble-free. Pests and diseases do not usually cause any problems

Gunnera manicata

Gunnera manicata

can then either be disposed of or trodden in around the plant to provide extra nutrients as they rot down. Flower spikes are often thrown up from the middle of the plant. They are huge, dark pink, and quite unmistakable.

G. manicata is suitable for any boggy area where the roots have unlimited access to plenty of water. They are excellent for planting around lakes and ponds or along riverbanks and streams, although even a small bog garden could perhaps accommodate one plant. It is important to remember, however, that although masses of water is required, this plant will not tolerate its roots permanently submerged in water, so it is quite unsuitable as an aquatic plant.

❄ *very hardy*

❄ Hebe parviflora angustifolia

A giant, evergreen cushion would sum up this plant in a nutshell. It is a round, soft-looking plant with long narrow leaves that stay bright emerald green year-round and, apart from its good looks, is immensely tough and very versatile. It can be grown in a wide range of conditions but is particularly useful for dry shade where very little else will grow. In full sun, it will keep its rounded shape with foliage down to the ground. In shade, the plant will be drawn up leaving it bare underneath and allowing it to take on the shape of a small tree with a lovely rounded top. It looks a bit like a miniature willow, with the added bonus of being evergreen. Because the foliage is so dense, *H. parviflora angustifolia* also makes a perfect hedge, which gets thicker the more it is clipped. Fuzzy gray-white flowers are produced in early summer—they do nothing to enhance this plant's appeal and can be removed if they cause visual offence.

The only place where this plant will not thrive is crammed into a small pot. It is fast growing and does not like having its roots

soil	Any soil. However, this plant must be grown in the ground and not put in a pot	
site	Sun or shade, although shelter from cold winds is desirable	
watering	Will cope with either being well watered or ignored	
general care	If grown as a hedge, clip little and often from mid-spring to late summer—don't cut into old wood	
pests & diseases	Generally trouble-free from pests and diseases, unless this Hebe is confined to a pot	

checked at all. Planting directly into the ground is essential, where dimensions can easily reach 7ft (2m) tall and wide in five years. It is a very easy plant to cultivate and fits into most planting schemes, being especially useful for planting beneath trees.

H

Hebe parviflora angustifolia

❄ Hedychium coccineum 'Tara'

Tara's
Ginger Lily

A tropical-looking perennial that gets bigger and better with age. The large, pointed leaves surround a thick fleshy stem, which can reach a height of 5ft (1.5m) during the growing season. The flowers are an unusual deep orange, lightly fragrant, and last for many weeks. The flower head is made up of dozens of individual blooms massed together in a cylindrical shape at the end of each stem. Bees adore them. The plants grow in clumps, which spread slowly, bulking up just a little bit more each year. They are best planted in groups of at least three, each trio will cover only one square yard (about one square meter) after five years. Flowering starts after three years, and the number of flower stems increases each year.

Once planted, these plants are best left undisturbed. Their life cycle starts in spring, when rhizomes are planted outside during late spring. They perform much better if planted directly into the ground, but a large container is an acceptable option. As soon as growth commences, constant watering will be required throughout the whole season to get good results. During the winter, plants that have been grown in pots should be tipped on their sides so that water drains out, keeping the rhizome dry until the following spring when growth

Hedychium coccineum 'Tara'

soil	Rich, loamy, and fertile. Well-drained conditions are vital	
site	Full sun or light shade in a sheltered spot. Will grow in a pot but better in the ground	
watering	Masses during growing season. During winter, let water drain out of pots	
general care	In colder areas, mulch the ground with straw in the winter for extra root protection	
pests & diseases	Outdoors, usually trouble-free. In a conservatory, red spider mite could become a problem	

recommences. These plants are very greedy and will consume as much food and water that is sent their way. However, the drainage must be first class so that water does not gather around the roots. Toward the end of late summer, stems will have reached their maximum height and odd lumpy-looking things will start to protrude. These will open up into flowers, which will be in their full glory between early and mid-fall. After this, the foliage will gradually turn yellow and die back. *H. coccineum* 'Tara' was discovered in the Himalayas in 1982 by the intrepid plant explorer Tony Schilling, and named in honor of his daughter.

❄ *hardy*

❄ Hedychium forrestii
Ginger Lily

This is not only one of the tallest Ginger Lilies but also one of the hardiest, suitable for most climates except for very cold, wet gardens. The leaves are dark green, large, and pointed. They encircle a central fleshy stem, which can reach a height of 7ft (2m) if optimum growing conditions are provided. The flowers are pure white and massed together to form a cylindrical shape at the end of each stem. They are a popular meeting place for the local bees. Too tall to keep confined to a pot, they should therefore be planted outside in groups directly into the soil for best effect. Choose the planting position carefully as they prefer to be left undisturbed. The rootstock increases in size each year, sending up more flowers annually as the plants mature. They are slow to spread out and can take many years to fill a good-sized space. The flowering season is from late summer until mid-fall. After this, the foliage starts to turn yellow and die down for the winter. They are slow to regrow the following year, often refusing to put in an appearance until late spring but once they start, growth is rapid, quickly reaching their full height. The typical lumpy growths that emerge from the stems and open up into flowers become noticeable during late summer.

Ginger Lilies make fantastically extravagant cut flowers—a bouquet of these not only looks wonderful, but would make any recipient quite weak at the knees.

These Chinese plants are fairly easy to propagate, although plants are so slow to bulk up that there is never much material to work with. The best time to do this is when a clump is just about to break its winter dormancy, sometime in late spring. Carefully slice the rootstock into pieces, making sure that there is at least one bud on each piece. Use a very sharp implement to cut with and, after cutting, rub some fungicide powder into each freshly cut surface. Pot each section up in some suitable potting mix and water sparingly until new growth appears.

To get the very best results from Ginger Lilies, rich growing conditions must be given, accompanied by large helpings of food and drink. They are among the greediest exotic plants that can be cultivated in colder climates.

Hedychium forrestii

soil		Rich, loamy, fertile, and well-drained soil is the best for this plant
site		Full sun or light shade in a sheltered spot. Too tall to be confined to a pot
watering		Masses required during growing season. Water must not collect around the roots
general care		Cut off old foliage when yellow and unsightly. Feed with generous amounts of well-rotted manure
pests & diseases		Relatively trouble-free. Pests and diseases do not usually cause any problems

❄ Helleborus foetidus

Stinking Hellebore

If the garden is shady and the soil is chalky, this evergreen plant is the perfect choice and should be planted in copious amounts. The leaves are finely cut, dark green, and glossy. Flowers are lime green and the flowering period lasts for several months, usually from early winter to mid-spring. Small plants grow rapidly to 2ft (60cm) and then stop, but each year the flower heads get larger. Mature flower stems can be smothered with over 150 flowers. Once plants are settled in, seeds are regularly produced and scattered all over the garden, so that small seedlings are found filling any spare space they

Helleborus foetidus

Helleborus foetidus

Helleborus foetidus

find. They are easily removed and not invasive enough to become a nuisance.

Although suitable for difficult planting sites, *H. foetidus* would still prefer to be in richer soil if it can be provided. Despite its common name, there is nothing unpleasant about the smell of the leaves or flowers. They can be planted in large drifts in shady borders or in groups underneath trees. They are also tolerant of seaside gardens and do not seem to mind being on the receiving end of the occasional blast of salty air. *H. foetidus* seems to have a reputation for being able to cure madness.

soil	Any—excellent in chalk, but fertile, well-drained loam is the favorite choice
site	Light to deep shade in either a sheltered or exposed position
watering	Prefers to be kept moist, but can manage perfectly well in dry conditions
general care	If the soil is poor, a light feed of blood, fish, and bone can be sprinkled around base during the growing season
pests & diseases	Check regularly for green aphids, which are often found on the flower heads during mild weather

❄ *very hardy*

Iris confusa
The Confused Iris

This plant is fully deserving of the common name of Confused Iris because it gives the distinct impression of not quite being able to make up its mind what it is. It does not look or behave as most irises would, but has characteristic traits of both bamboo and palm tree. The stems are definitely reminiscent of a bamboo, being quite hard and woody. These grow to around 60cm (2ft) in height. They are topped by what looks like a type of palm leaf with fronds that are about 8in (20cm) across made up of individual "fingers" that are broad and flat. They are fully evergreen and hardy if sited correctly. The flowers are of secondary interest, but are delicate and quite pleasing to the eye.

soil	Thrives in any type of soil that is fertile and thoroughly well drained
site	Full sun in a sheltered spot. Light shade tends to produce fewer flowers
watering	Happy in dryish conditions unless grown in a pot, where it will need regular irrigation
general care	Remove yellowing leaves, cutting them off as near to the base as possible. Feeding not usually necessary
pests & diseases	*Iris confusa* is a magnet for every slug in the vicinity and the use of a slug repellent is essential

Iris confusa

They are long-lasting and appear during mid- to late spring. Their color is white, tinged slightly with mauve and the occasional yellow mark along the petals.

I. confusa prefers full sun and sharp drainage. The plant does well if it is planted at the base of a sun-baked wall, so that extra heat is reflected from the bricks behind. Soil at the base of such walls also tends to be drier, which suits these plants admirably. They do quite well if grown in pots provided that the containers are at least 18in (45cm) across, but preferably bigger. These plants are very popular with slugs and will take a battering unless they are fully protected with repellent.

Iris confusa

 hardy

❄ Kniphofia caulescens

Red Hot Poker

There are many different types of kniphofia available and all of them seem to share the same common name of Red Hot Poker, which describes the flowers beautifully but could lead to confusion unless the Latin name is strictly adhered to. Many kniphofias are grown for their flowers alone, but occasionally the foliage is special enough to be the main attraction. *K. caulescens* is certainly in this category. Lovely rosettes of blue-gray foliage give it the kind of tropical appearance that some of the yuccas have, but without the sharp bits. It is a slow plant to get going, but gradually the rosettes send up more baby plants from the base, which spread to form larger clumps. They are tough, fully hardy, and evergreen. Woody stems 2ft (60cm)

long are sent up from the center of each mature rosette every fall. These open out into tubular flowers massed together to form a cylindrical shape that is fiery orange-red at the tip and yellow underneath. They last for many weeks.

K. caulescens is happy at the front of a border or kept in a pot blending in well with most planting schemes. It looks splendid planted into gravel gardens.

This is an easy plant to cultivate as it can cope with a wide variety of soil types. However, although poor, thin soil can be tolerated, much better results will be achieved by applying generous amounts of well-rotted manure around the base annually during late spring.

As *Kniphofia caulescens* can take a long time to fill a good-sized space, it is better to

Kniphofia caulescens

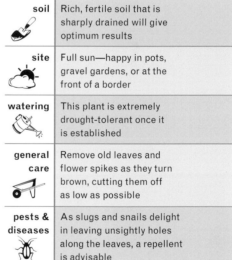

soil	Rich, fertile soil that is sharply drained will give optimum results
site	Full sun—happy in pots, gravel gardens, or at the front of a border
watering	This plant is extremely drought-tolerant once it is established
general care	Remove old leaves and flower spikes as they turn brown, cutting them off as low as possible
pests & diseases	As slugs and snails delight in leaving unsightly holes along the leaves, a repellent is advisable

plant them in groups of at least five to start with, as a single specimen would take many years to create any impact.

Propagation of these lovely South African plants can be done easily by division, but as suitable material is slow to develop, growing them from fresh seed is by far the best option. These plants get their rather difficult name from Johann Hieronymus Kniphof, a Professor of Medicine and a plant illustrator, in whose honor they were first named.

 ❄ *very hardy*

❄ Kniphofia northiae

Red Hot Poker

A massive kniphofia—the biggest and chunkiest one of all. The evergreen leaves are wide, curving straps, up to 5ft (1.5m) long and edged with small, sharp serrations that run down the whole length. Short, stubby stems form the base of each rosette, giving the whole plant the appearance of a giant pot leek. They rarely grow as clumps, preferring to put all of their energy into one massive, solitary specimen. The height can be as much as 3ft (1m).

Short, rather squat flower spikes appear during the fall. These open out into a torch-shaped bloom that is made up of coral red flowers on the top and creamy yellow ones underneath. These lovely South African beasts fit beautifully into any architectural garden, whether it is jungly, spiky, or flowery. They look wonderful in gravel gardens and can sit quite happily for several years in large terracotta pots.

K. northiae are greedy plants that need lots of food and water. In their native country, they are seen growing in large colonies along streams and riverbanks, where they have access to a constant supply of water. They are nearly always found on a sloping site, so that any excess rain can run away without it collecting around the roots. The conditions that they enjoy in the wild should be mimicked exactly in cultivation to achieve the same

Kniphofia northiae

vast proportions. Once planted out, they loathe root disturbance and transplant badly, so choose their planting position carefully so that they can spend their entire life in one place.

Kniphofia northiae

soil	Rich, fertile, and free-draining conditions are ideal for this plant
site	Full sun in a sheltered spot, where protection from strong winds can be given
watering	Masses of water during growing season for new plants and those in pots
general care	These plants appreciate large dollops of well-rotted manure applied annually during late spring
pests & diseases	Slugs delight in scraping off the surface of the leaves, leaving large grazed areas and causing serious damage

❄ *very hardy*

Lampranthus spectabilis

Fast-growing ground cover with rubbery leaves and glorious magenta flowers. *L. spectabilis* is a hardy succulent that grows thickly to provide a dense matt, which is the perfect foil for all larger spiky plants. It complements agaves, dasylirions, and yuccas brilliantly, making it excellent undergrowth for desert gardens. It also looks perfectly at home when used as underplanting in Mediterranean gardens, contrasting particularly well with palms. This plant adores hot, sunny, sharply drained aspects and can be used to cover sloping banks and rockeries or left to cascade down over walls and the edges of large stone troughs. Roughly one square foot (30 square centimeters) of this tough evergreen can increase tenfold with ease after two years of planting. The large daisy flowers open up during the summer when the weather is sunny.

Lampranthus spectabilis thrives in any soil that is gritty and well drained, but although poor soil is acceptable, an occasional light feed with a small amount of blood, fish, and bone scattered around the edge of the clump gives good results. Feed during mid- to late spring, taking care not to get any of the plant food on the delicate foliage. As an extra precaution, hose down the plant and water in the food immediately after its application to prevent scorching. Watering is not usually required and the plants can largely take care of themselves, relying on surplus stores of water hoarded in their fleshy leaves.

Mature plants can become a bit straggly, so trim back the ends hard to encourage new bushier tips. The bits that have been cut off can be used for propagation. Alternatively, these plants can easily be raised from fresh seed. These plants are native to South Africa and are a frequent sight in the Cape Province.

Lampranthus spectabilis

soil	These plants will thrive in any soil that is gritty and very well drained
site	Full sun is preferred and can cope well with exposed coastal conditions
watering	Water in new plants for first few weeks. Very drought-resistant once established
general care	A light feed with a small amount of blood, fish, and bone in late spring or early summer gives good results
pests & diseases	*Lampranthus spectabilis* is generally trouble-free from most pests and diseases

❄ *hardy*

❄ Libertia formosa

A gentle, well-behaved perennial with tufts of grassy leaves that emerge from a central clump. These flat, evergreen leaves grow to about 2ft (60cm) in length and are sent up in numerous quantities, making the plant more substantial with each growing season. The whole plant has the appearance of a miniature phormium. Tall flower spikes emerge from the center during mid-spring and are usually fully open by late spring. Each spike consists of wiry stems adorned with many clusters of orchid-like tri-petaled flowers that are bright white with yellow stamens. They last for many weeks. A mature *L. formosa* can be several feet (nearly a meter) across and a plant this size will produce around 30–40 flower stems per year.

Although much better quality plants are always produced if they are planted directly into the ground, *L. formosa* is better than most for giving good results if confined to a terracotta pot, where it can remain relatively content for several years. This plant originates from Chile and the name *formosa* is the Latin word meaning handsome.

soil	Will grow anywhere, but light, loamy soil is preferred—soil-based potting mix if in a pot
site	This plant enjoys full sun to light shade in a sheltered position
watering	Once established, very little irrigation is required. In a pot, watering always needed
general care	An annual feed with blood, fish, and bone in spring would be beneficial. Remove any older, yellow-brown leaves
pests & diseases	Rarely a problem, apart from checking for the occasional aphid on the ends of the flower buds

Libertia formosa

Libertia formosa

❄ *hardy*

✳ Lobelia tupa
Devil's Tobacco

A huge perennial herb that can reach 7ft (2m) tall and is at its most striking when planted in large numbers. The large, towering spikes consist of thick stems, which are covered with soft foliage on the bottom half, and have a magnificent spire of flowers on the top half. Leaves are pointed, downy, and 10in (25cm) long. The flowers, which appear during mid-summer, are made up of hundreds of tubular blooms that are deep red in color. They are the perfect shape to be pollinated by the long beaks of the hummingbirds that live along the hilly coastal regions of Chile where this plant grows wild.

Despite its size, *L. tupa* stands up well against sea breezes, making it a good choice for a coastal garden. It also fits in with most other styles of gardening, but it is hopeless in a pot and must be planted

soil	*Lobelia tupa* enjoys rich, moist, fertile, and free-draining soil
site	Full sun or light shade. Must be planted in the ground as it is hopeless in a pot
watering	Water plants well during growing season from late spring until early fall
general care	Remove dead flower spikes when they turn brown. Feed with well-rotted manure annually in early spring
pests & diseases	Make regular checks for green aphids, as these can be a problem on the growing tips

directly into the ground as soon as it is large enough to handle. Small plants are best introduced to the garden in the spring when that year's frosts have finished, usually around late spring time. In their first year, they will grow about 3–4ft (1m) and then flower during mid-summer. It is during their second year, when they have become established, that their full stature develops. Growth starts again rapidly in early spring and by mid-summer the full height of 7ft (2m) should have been reached if growing conditions are right.

This plant grows throughout most of the year, continuing well into the fall. Leaves then start to become a bit brown and shabby, and stems should then be cut right down to the base. New growth can start again as early as mid-winter during mild weather, so there won't be much of a gap in the garden for very long.

Although these plants bulk up and spread slightly after a few years, planting just one or two is not enough, and larger groups of at least five look much more dramatic. The common name refers to the fact that if huge numbers are chopped back in the confined conditions of a small glasshouse, the air around them can become toxic. In normal conditions outside, this would not be a problem.

Lobelia tupa

Other Leafy Exotics

L

✳ *hardy*

❊ Mahonia lomariifolia

Of all the many types of mahonia available, *M. lomariifolia* is by far the most imposing, being much more delicate and far less loutish than the more commonly grown varieties. This large, evergreen, and supremely architectural shrub could reach 10ft (3m) in ten years. It has thick, corky stems, each one ending in a flourish of wide-spreading foliage made up of many pairs of spiny leaves that look a bit like holly. Large clusters of bright yellow flowers appear at various times of the year, but usually during late fall. They are lightly fragrant, and are followed by bunches of blue-black fruits.

Although a fine shrub if left to grow naturally, it can be hugely improved with a pair of pruners. Whenever the stem is cut on a young plant, more foliage will appear. With this in mind, try to create a plant that consists of five or six stems, all of different heights and all topped with a head of foliage that has enough room to spread out fully, without being entangled with its neighbor. From a distance and with a bit of imagination,

Mahonia lomariifolia

the whole plant can resemble a mini grove of palm trees. Warm weather in early spring can produce new growth, which is easily scorched by late frosts. If new growth becomes blackened, cut it off—it will soon send out new replacement shoots.

Mahonia lomariifolia

soil	The soil must be rich, moist, and fertile for this plant to thrive
site	Light woodland shade under trees and sheltered from cold winds is the ideal spot
watering	Should not be allowed to dry out for first 2–3 years, then usually takes care of itself
general care	A good helping of well-rotted manure annually each spring is important, especially if grown on poorer soils
pests & diseases	*Mahonia lomariifolia* is generally trouble-free from most pests and diseases

❊ *hardy*

❄ Melianthus major

Honey Flower *or* Honey Bush

A highly decorative perennial with huge, deeply cut foliage. The leaves are beautifully sculpted, pale blue-gray in color, and exude a strong smell of peanut butter when they are touched. A height of at least 5ft (1.5m) can be reached in one year, with most of the growth occurring from early to late fall. Mature plants send up tall flower spikes, which are best described as interesting and spectacular, rather than beautiful. The spikes soar above the foliage and open up into slender cone shapes that are colored blood red. The flowering period

soil	Rich, moist, and fertile. Well-drained loam would be ideal conditions
site	Full sun or light shade in a sheltered spot away from strong winds
watering	Moist conditions are preferred in order to provide continuous growth
general care	Remove older leaves when they get brown and crispy. Stems are delicate, so use pruners to make clean cuts
pests & diseases	Usually problem-free from diseases and pests if grown outdoors and planted directly into the ground

Melianthus major

is usually around early summer. The outer parts of the flowers contain a honey-like substance, hence the common name of Honey Flower. The size and color of the leaves contrast well with virtually all other architectural plants, whether they are trees, bamboos, or herbaceous.

M. major is not very hardy and is often cut back to the ground by frosts, but as the growth on older plants can sometimes become leggy, hard pruning is no bad thing. The new growth that follows a severe hacking is much improved, giving extra bushiness to the entire shape. Cut brown, older leaves off with pruners, instead of tugging at them. The stems are delicate and could snap with rough treatment. If pruned back to the ground, new growth can take a while to reappear. Don't give up on it, however, as it nearly always recovers. This plant is hopeless in a pot unless grown in a truly gigantic container.

Melianthus major

❄ *tender*

✳ Musa basjoo

Japanese Banana

The most absurd-looking exotic tropical plant that can be grown in colder climates— a plant that often makes the neighbors question your sanity. No one believes there really is such a thing as a hardy banana, but there is and this is it. With the right growing conditions, *M. basjoo* can easily reach 7ft (2m) in one year and can eventually grow as tall as 20ft (6m). Huge leaves can be produced at the rate of one per week at the height of the growing season. These unfurl to reveal a large "paddle," which is bright vivid green and 6ft (1.8m) long. Leaves grow from a base that eventually forms a fibrous, watery trunk. Suckers are produced from around this base, which grow to form a small grove of extra plants. These can be cut off, but look much better if left to grow as a multistemmed clump. Mature stems can produce flowers, which are large and lumpy and extend from a curved stalk. Behind the flower bud, tiny bunches of bananas appear. These are hard, green, and inedible but to have these growing in a nontropical climate always brings on a feeling of total disbelief. They are truly amazing. This stem dies after fruiting, but sends up new plants from the roots to replace it. Frost always destroys the foliage. In milder gardens, the trunk stays hardy through the winter and new growth starts from the top the following year. In colder areas the trunk can be left for the frost to kill and new growth will appear from the base the following year in late spring. Alternatively, the

soil	This plant thrives best in soil that is rich, moist, and fertile	
site	Light shade preferred in a sheltered spot to protect the fragile leaves from the wind	
watering	Vast amounts required throughout the entire growing season	
general care	Feed every 4 weeks from mid-spring to mid-summer—lots of well-rotted manure or a mix of blood, fish, and bone	
pests & diseases	Not usually a problem unless plant is stressed by being forced to grow in a pot rather than in the ground	

Musa basjoo

Musa basjoo

trunk can be wrapped for the winter. (This is fully explained on pages 20–21.) By doing this, it remains alive all winter and new growth will then sprout from the top. This not only produces bigger plants, but also allows it to become mature enough to fruit and flower.

M

Other Leafy Exotics

❄ Phormium cookianum

Mountain Flax

Sword-shaped, evergreen leaves grow from fan-shaped bases in copious amounts to create clumps roughly 4ft (1.2m) tall and the same wide within three years. The number of leaves on a plant this size could be at least 150, making a strongly architectural shape for the garden. Flower spikes are sent up from the center during the summer. They are slightly taller than the foliage, and would be referred to as interesting rather than items of stunning loveliness. They open out into large yellowish-green angular blooms and when these fade, seed pods begin to form, which are much more attractive than the flowers and should be left on the plant to enjoy visually. They are long-lasting and much admired. *P. cookianum* is a plant of varying hardiness—some forms are worthy of the green hardiness color code, but the provenance of these should be checked thoroughly before planting out in extremely cold climates. It is sometimes still listed under the synonym of *P. colensoi*. The variegated form, *P. cookianum* 'Tricolor', has striking leaves of cream and green with subtle red edges. It is not only attractive, but just as hardy as the green version. The

Phormium cookianum

soil	Fertile and free-draining. In frost-prone areas, supply a deep, dry mulch
site	Full sun or light shade—excellent in exposed coastal gardens
watering	Water well for first season. Watering then needed only in periods of drought
general care	Feed annually with blood, fish, and bone. Don't plant central base too low—water gathers, leading to rotting
pests & diseases	Mealy bug can be a problem, but apart from this pest the plant is relatively trouble-free

market is flooded with many named cultivars, most of which will lose their bright colors within a couple of years and are perhaps best regarded as only temporary additions to the garden. An exception to this is *Phormium* 'Yellow Wave', which manages to hold its lime green and yellow colors well. Plants that have highly colored foliage are often difficult to place harmoniously in planting schemes and rarely succeed in being pleasing to the eye.

Phormium cookianum

❄ *hardy*

Phormium tenax

New Zealand Flax

Massive sword-shaped leaves up to 7ft (2m) tall grow from fan-shaped bases to create enormous clumps of upright foliage. A mature clump could be 8ft (2.5m) across within six years. It is an easy plant to cultivate and has been the basis for many architectural gardens for years. The flower spikes are extraordinary—they tower over the foliage by many feet and open up into angular, reddish-brown flowers, similar in shape to the bird-of-paradise plant. The flowers still manage to look attractive even when they are dead and their color has faded and turned black. The variegated version, *P. tenax* 'Variegatum', is worthy of a mention even though it is slightly less hardy. This grows to 6ft (1.8m) tall. There is also a good purple variety, *P. tenax purpureum*, which is even less hardy and grows to around 5ft (1.5m) tall.

There are hundreds of other named cultivars available, all with brightly colored foliage and all with rather absurd names such as 'Bronze Baby', 'Apricot Queen', and 'Dusky Maiden'. Few are hardy

	soil	Fertile and free-draining. In frost-prone areas, supply a deep, dry mulch
	site	Full sun or light shade is the best—excellent in exposed coastal gardens
	watering	Water well for first season. Irrigation then needed only in periods of drought
	general care	Feed annually with blood, fish, and bone. Don't plant central base too low—water gathers, leading to rotting
	pests & diseases	Mealy bug can be a problem, but apart from this pest the plant is relatively trouble-free

Phormium tenax

Phormium tenax

and within two years most of them will either be dead or have reverted to a mucky brown color. They are probably best regarded as temporary bedding plants only and discarded at the end of each season. The loud colors are often difficult to place and can disturb the otherwise peaceful tranquility of a tasteful architectural planting scheme.

❄ *very hardy*

✲ Pittosporum tobira

Japanese Mock Orange

P

Other Leafy Exotics

The delicious scent from the flowers that appear during early summer is just one of many reasons for growing this hardy evergreen. *P. tobira* is one of the most versatile plants available. It can be trained as a small tree, clipped into a hedge, or left as a shapely shrub. There is even a dwarf form that can be grown successfully in a pot. The leaves are dark and leathery and look as though they have been recently sprayed with leafshine. The ultimate height is not usually more than 8ft (2.5m). Flowers are borne in clusters during late spring and early summer, and have a heady perfume reminiscent of gardenia. They are pale, creamy-white when they first open and gradually change to butter-yellow as they age. After a hot summer, the flowers are followed by bunches of green seed pods the size and shape of cob nuts. When ripe, these split open to reveal bright orange seeds, which remain on the plant for many weeks. There is a variegated form available, which has beautiful silvery-cream markings on

the leaves. Unfortunately, it is not reliably hardy except in very mild areas.

P. tobira is fantastically salt-resistant and makes an excellent addition to a coastal garden, especially when grown as a long, fragrant hedge. It can be quite a difficult plant to position—lots of sun produces masses of flowers, whereas if grown in the shade, the foliage becomes larger and looks healthier, glossier, and a stronger color. Somewhere between the two is what to aim for. Just before the new growth starts in the spring, older leaves can become yellow and drop off in alarming amounts. This is all perfectly normal and, provided that this phase lasts no more than a few weeks, there is nothing to worry about.

Pittosporum tobira

Pittosporum tobira

soil	Any, but grows best in soil that is fertile, moist, and well drained	
site	Sun or shade—excellent in exposed windy gardens, especially on the coast	
watering	Once established this plant is wonderfully drought-resistant	
general care	The pruning of shaped plants or hedging should be done in early spring or right after flowering	
pests & diseases	Black aphids can be a menace to new shoots and flower buds, so check regularly for these pests	

✲ *hardy*

❄ Rosmarinus repens

Creeping Rosemary

At last! A ground cover rosemary that not only grows lush and dense, but is hardy as well. Thick, bushy growth hugs the ground and provides the perfect underblanket for sunny Mediterranean-style gardens. The fragrance from the crushed leaves is unbeatable and the pretty mauve flowers can appear sporadically on the previous year's growth throughout the year, although late spring is the main flowering time. It looks good if allowed to crawl over gravel or left to

soil		Poor, sandy soil is best but is happy growing anywhere with sharp drainage
site		Full sun—wonderful for coastal gardens as it copes brilliantly with salty winds
watering		Generally self-sufficient once established. Excellent drought resistance
general care		Feeding is usually unnecessary. Pruning the leaf tips keeps the whole plant even more bushy
pests & diseases		*Rosmarinus repens* is generally trouble-free from most pests and diseases

Rosmarinus repens

hang over the edges of pots, troughs, and walls. The strongly aromatic leaves can still be used for culinary purposes in exactly the same way as any other rosemary. Unfortunately, this plant is not very long-lived. Older plants are not only less vigorous, but seem to be slightly less hardy, too.

There is much confusion over the naming of this plant. *R. lavandulaceus* is similar, but has more vigorous growth and woodier stems, which makes it unsuitable for small pots or troughs. *R. prostratus* also looks similar but is far less hardy.

Rosmarinus repens

❄ *hardy*

✳ Tetrapanax papyrifera
Rice Paper Plant

A large, evergreen shrub or small tree that is rather unruly, wilfully refusing to grow straight. The leaves are enormous, up to 1ft (30cm) across and deeply lobed. They are lightly covered with a white powder that is quite harmless, although occasionally it causes violently loud sneezing if too much is inhaled. The long stems are filled with pith, which is used for making Chinese rice paper.

This plant stays as a shrub, growing quite neatly for some years. Then, as the lower leaves age and drop off, a trunk is revealed giving it the appearance of a small tree. The trunk is gnarled and twisted, and the overall height of a mature plant can be up to 20ft (6m). It is an essential addition to any jungly garden. Flowers are produced in

Tetrapanax papyrifera

the fall. They are long and cream in color. The flowers are passably attractive, but can be removed if preferred, so conserving all the plant's energy for the splendid foliage. In colder areas, the foliage will always be cut back by the frost, but as long as it is planted directly into the ground, the plant usually regenerates from the roots each spring. If *T. papyrifera* becomes too tall and leggy, it can be pruned back hard in late spring.

There are several forms of this plant available, some much hardier than others. However, unless the exact form being purchased is known, it is best to assume they are not likely to be reliably frost-resistant. It is sometimes listed in nursery catalogs as *Aralia papyrifera* or *Fatsia papyrifera*.

Tetrapanax papyrifera

soil	Rich, heavy, moist soil preferred—does very well in clay
site	Light shade in a sheltered spot away from the wind, which can tear large leaves
watering	Does not like to dry out, should be watered regularly in its first few seasons
general care	Large helpings of well-rotted manure applied in mid-spring benefits this plant enormously
pests & diseases	Capsid bug can be a nuisance, ruining the leaves. Green aphids are also fond of the new shoots

✳ *tender*

❋ Zantedeschia aethiopica 'Crowborough'

Calla Lily

Big, leafy herbaceous plant with large jungly leaves up to 2ft (60cm) long and 1ft (30cm) across. The flowers are a delight— enormous pure white trumpets with a real look of the tropics about them. This is a clump-forming plant that increases in width each year, although the height rarely exceeds 3ft (90cm). They look particularly effective if planted in large groups along the banks of ponds or streams, where they can have constant access to water, for which they have an almost insatiable thirst. In very mild gardens, they can be planted directly into a pond or lake margin, provided that the water never freezes and the water is at least 1ft (30cm) deep so that the rhizome stays a good distance away from any frost. Shelter from strong winds is advisable. They are fairly successful if grown in containers, but the watering during the summer has to be done so frequently that it can become a real chore.

Zantedeschia aethiopica 'Crowborough'

soil		Very rich, heavily manured soil is the preferred option for this plant
site		Sun or shade, but light shade gives the leaves a rich, bright green color
watering		Copious amounts of water should be given throughout the growing season
general care		Remove older leaves as they become discolored, until cut down to ground level—will grow back after winter
pests & diseases		Despite their very appetizing-looking leaves, they seem to be remarkably trouble-free

There are many calla lilies available, but the 'Crowborough' variety seems to be hardier than the others and more forgiving of less than ideal growing conditions. The plants die down each winter, with the foliage gradually becoming more yellow and unattractive. Remove these older leaves as they become discolored, cutting down to ground level.

Z

Troubleshooting

Growing a varied range of plants attracts an equally varied selection of pests, diseases, and other problems. The following diagram is designed to help you diagnose problems with your plants from the symptoms you can observe. Starting with the part of the plant that appears to be most affected—stems, leaves, or general cultivation problems—by answering successive questions "yes" [✓] or "no" [✗] you will quickly arrive at a probable cause. Once you have identified the cause, turn to the relevant entry in the directory of pests and diseases for details of how to treat the problem.

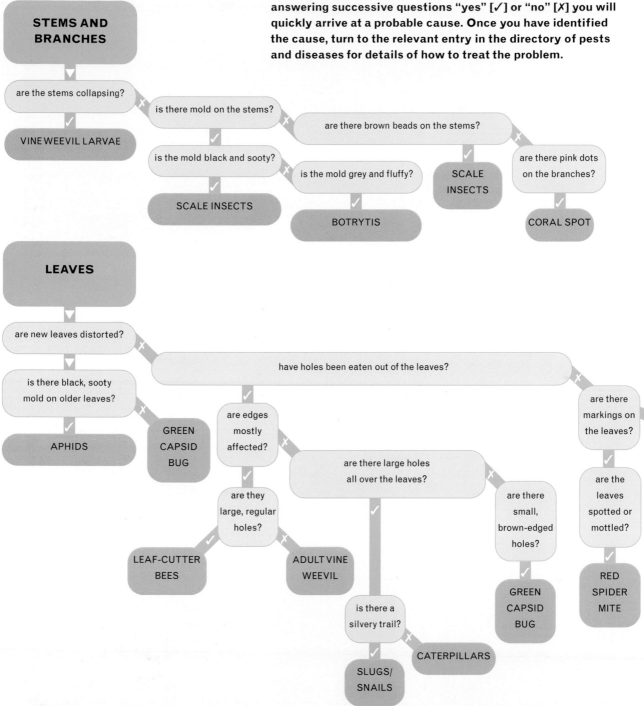

STEMS AND BRANCHES

are the stems collapsing?

VINE WEEVIL LARVAE

is there mold on the stems?

are there brown beads on the stems?

is the mold black and sooty?

is the mold grey and fluffy?

SCALE INSECTS

are there pink dots on the branches?

SCALE INSECTS

BOTRYTIS

CORAL SPOT

LEAVES

are new leaves distorted?

have holes been eaten out of the leaves?

are there markings on the leaves?

is there black, sooty mold on older leaves?

APHIDS

GREEN CAPSID BUG

are edges mostly affected?

are there large holes all over the leaves?

are there small, brown-edged holes?

are the leaves spotted or mottled?

are they large, regular holes?

LEAF-CUTTER BEES

ADULT VINE WEEVIL

GREEN CAPSID BUG

RED SPIDER MITE

is there a silvery trail?

CATERPILLARS

SLUGS/ SNAILS

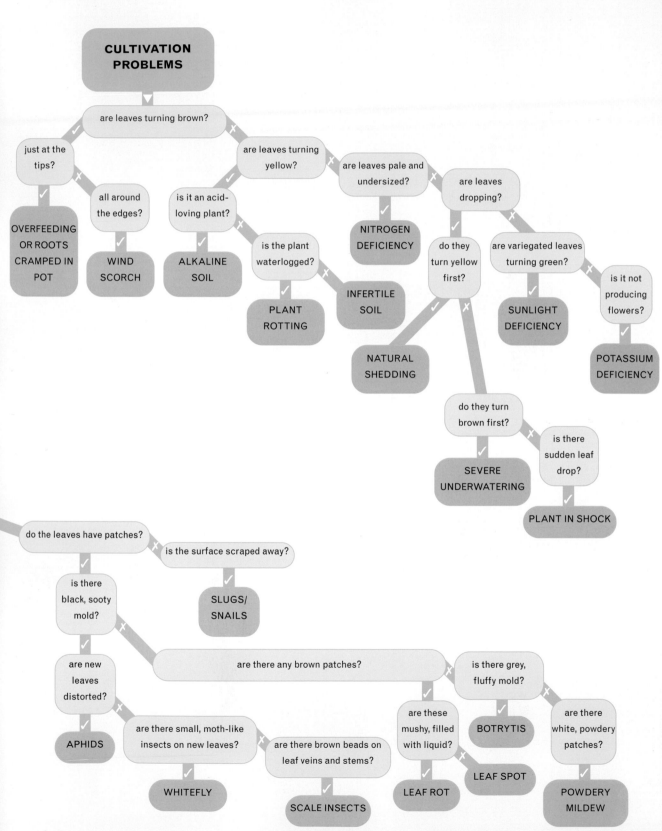

CULTIVATION PROBLEMS

are leaves turning brown?

just at the tips? → OVERFEEDING OR ROOTS CRAMPED IN POT

all around the edges? → WIND SCORCH

are leaves turning yellow?

is it an acid-loving plant? → ALKALINE SOIL

is the plant waterlogged? → PLANT ROTTING

INFERTILE SOIL

are leaves pale and undersized? → NITROGEN DEFICIENCY

are leaves dropping?

do they turn yellow first? → NATURAL SHEDDING

are variegated leaves turning green? → SUNLIGHT DEFICIENCY

is it not producing flowers? → POTASSIUM DEFICIENCY

do they turn brown first? → SEVERE UNDERWATERING

is there sudden leaf drop? → PLANT IN SHOCK

do the leaves have patches?

is the surface scraped away? → SLUGS/SNAILS

is there black, sooty mold?

are new leaves distorted? → APHIDS

are there any brown patches?

are there small, moth-like insects on new leaves? → WHITEFLY

are there brown beads on leaf veins and stems? → SCALE INSECTS

are these mushy, filled with liquid? → LEAF ROT

is there grey, fluffy mold? → BOTRYTIS

LEAF SPOT

are there white, powdery patches? → POWDERY MILDEW

153

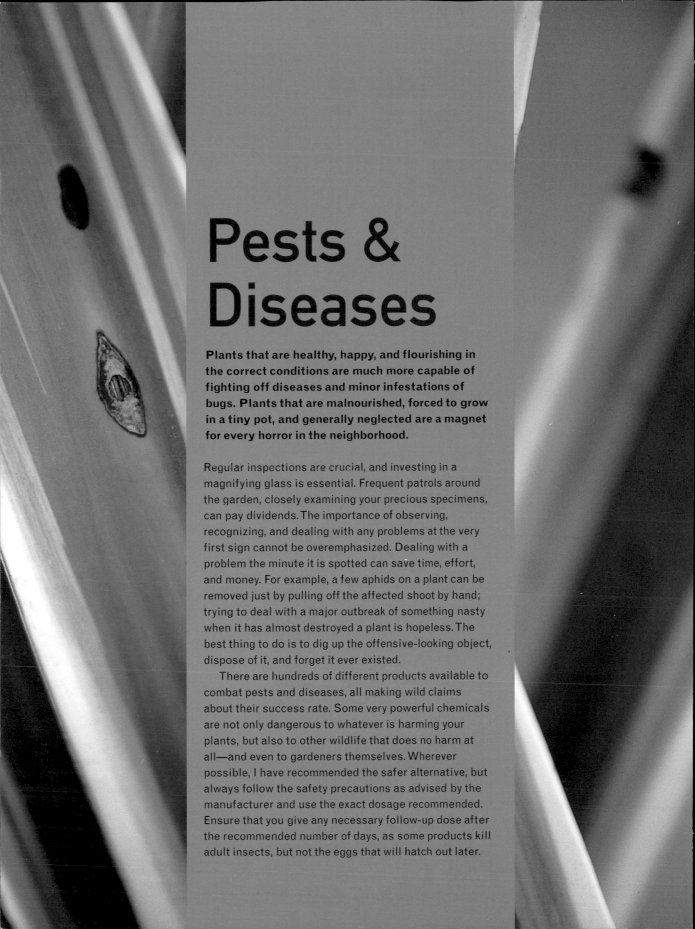

Pests & Diseases

Plants that are healthy, happy, and flourishing in the correct conditions are much more capable of fighting off diseases and minor infestations of bugs. Plants that are malnourished, forced to grow in a tiny pot, and generally neglected are a magnet for every horror in the neighborhood.

Regular inspections are crucial, and investing in a magnifying glass is essential. Frequent patrols around the garden, closely examining your precious specimens, can pay dividends. The importance of observing, recognizing, and dealing with any problems at the very first sign cannot be overemphasized. Dealing with a problem the minute it is spotted can save time, effort, and money. For example, a few aphids on a plant can be removed just by pulling off the affected shoot by hand; trying to deal with a major outbreak of something nasty when it has almost destroyed a plant is hopeless. The best thing to do is to dig up the offensive-looking object, dispose of it, and forget it ever existed.

There are hundreds of different products available to combat pests and diseases, all making wild claims about their success rate. Some very powerful chemicals are not only dangerous to whatever is harming your plants, but also to other wildlife that does no harm at all—and even to gardeners themselves. Wherever possible, I have recommended the safer alternative, but always follow the safety precautions as advised by the manufacturer and use the exact dosage recommended. Ensure that you give any necessary follow-up dose after the recommended number of days, as some products kill adult insects, but not the eggs that will hatch out later.

Aphids

Aphids feed on the young growth of a plant, spreading virus and depositing a sticky substance that can cause black, sooty mold. Bamboos, Pittosporums, bananas, Arbutus, Cupressus, and Yucca flowers are especially prone to aphid attack. Apply organic insecticide regularly throughout the growing season. Ladybugs and their larvae feed on destructive pests such as aphids, so do not discourage them from your garden.

Green capsid

The sign of green capsid infestation is tiny, reddish-brown spots on the plant, which expand to produce numerous holes in the leaves. The toxic saliva of the capsid bug kills plant tissues, causing the leaves to eventually tear. Damage is not usually apparent until the insects have long gone. *Euphorbia mellifera* and *Paulownia tomentosa* are favorite choices of this bug. Apply organic insecticide regularly on plants likely to be attacked as a precautionary measure.

Whitefly

Although common in glasshouses, these pests can also occur frequently during hot weather on Arbutus, Phillyrea, Lyonothamnus, and Clematis. They feed on sap and deposit a sticky substance that can lead to black, sooty mold. They can breed to form enormous numbers in an alarmingly short time. Whitefly can produce a new generation every three days, so the frequent and regular use of insecticide is more important than what is applied. The organic spray used for aphids and capsid bugs, as above, is as good as any.

Vine weevil

Adults can nibble the leaves, but the main damage done is by the larvae that live in the soil and feed on the roots, causing the plant to collapse. Container plants are particularly vulnerable, especially Echeverias, Aloes, and ferns. Wander around the garden with a flashlight at night, squashing any adults found; or use a suitable vine weevil killer liquid. Mix it up and water into each pot during the growing season. This will give six months' protection against the larvae and will kill any adults that touch the plant for up to four weeks.

Mealy bug

White, furry masses of insects that cling to the plant and feed off the sap. Phormiums, agaves, and other succulents are the most likely plants to attract these pests. Small numbers can be removed with a cotton swab dipped into methylated spirits (rubbing alcohol). Ladybugs love this pest during the warmer months. However, large colonies need a strong systemic insecticidal chemical, sprayed at fortnightly intervals.

Slugs & snails

These creatures usually come out at night to feed, or after rainfall, leaving a silvery slime trail in their wake and heavily eaten leaves as evidence of their visit the following morning. Slugs and snails enjoy eating most plants. As animals such as frogs feed on slugs and snails, it is important not to poison them. Try to avoid using organic mulches, which encourage them to come into your garden. To attempt to control slugs and snails, either go outside at night to collect any seen in the garden, which may prevent the build-up of eggs, or use pellets that contain a slug repellent rather than a slug killer, which will not harm beneficial wildlife.

Leaf-cutter bees

Large, semi-circular pieces of leaves are sliced from the margins of the leaf of trees such as Arbutus and other trees and shrubs, and used by the bees in the construction of their nests. The damage these creatures cause is usually slight and they are useful for pollination, so there is no need to harm them—unless plants are heavily damaged, control is not necessary. However, if they are a persistent nuisance, the only thing you could try is swatting them as they return back to chew their lozenge-shaped pieces out of the leaf.

Scale insects

There are many different types of scale insect damage, but the brown scale variety is the most commonly found. It takes the form of brown "beads" fixed along the stems and leaves. *Laurus nobilis angustifolia*, and *Olea europea* are very prone to this. They should be scraped off at the very first sign, which is normally early to mid-summer for plants grown outside and year-round on plants grown under glass. They feed on the sap, do a great deal of harm, and breed very fast. Severely affected plants should be disposed of.

Leaf spot

This is commonly found in plants such as Arbutus, Yuccas, Eriobotrya, and Chamaerops. It is a type of fungal disease and can spread through entire plants. Remove affected leaves at the first sign and burn them. Routinely drench any plants likely to suffer from this with a systemic fungicide containing copper, and improve drainage. Cold, wet winters will increase the frequency of leaf spots.

Botrytis

The more common name or description of Botrytis is grey mold. This fluffy mold is more likely to affect plants grown under glass, but could be a problem to soft-leafed plants outside, such as *Melianthus major* and *Musa basjoo*. Try to avoid injuring the whole plant; provide good air circulation if grown under glass and ensure that the plants are adequately spaced. Pick off affected leaves or stems and burn them immediately as this could spread through the whole plant and kill it.

Coral spot

This infection manifests itself as pink fungal spots, more commonly found on dead wood and bark, although it can affect living shoots as well. *Albizia julibrissin* is a plant frequently affected. Saw off any affected branches to well below the obviously infected region and regularly remove any dead wood. All diseased wood should be burned.

Sooty mold

This is usually found growing on the excretions of insects such as aphids, scale insects, and whitefly. Although insects should be dealt with before this stage is reached, the same treatment for the aforementioned pests should be applied here. Remove any blackened leaves. As a preventive measure, organic insecticide should be regularly applied throughout the growing season. Ladybugs and their larvae feed on such destructive pests, so do not discourage them from your garden.

Red spider mite

These can affect almost anything but are rarely found on plants outside. The main symptom is a yellow mottling on leaves, and in severe cases small webs appear between the top leaves within which the mites can be seen as tiny red dots. An infestation can be treated by applying a chemical spray such as malathion, which may need to be done up to twice a week. However, a much better option is to use biological control by introducing natural insect predators—the best is *Phytoseilus persimilis*—available by mail order. Prevention is the best remedy, however. As mites flourish in a hot, dry environment it is a good idea to increase humidity and improve ventilation where the plants are growing.

Powdery mildew

This type of disease is a white, powdery patch that appears on the leaves of shrubs, mainly on the upper surface but sometimes on both sides, usually appearing after a dry winter. Euonymus and Mahonia can be particularly susceptible to attack from this disease. Treat by removing the affected areas immediately. Then spray the whole plant thoroughly with a fungicide recommended by your local garden center. If the problem persists, use the fungicide again one week later, then every four weeks as a preventive precaution.

Rotting

Agaves, succulents, and yuccas can suffer from rot during a very wet winter. Remove affected leaves before the rot spreads through the plant. In the fall, drench each plant with a copper-based fungicide to try to prevent this occurring throughout the winter months. Ensure that the plant has sufficient drainage, and add gravel or shingle to help if necessary. This preparation should be available from most good garden centers.

Yellowing/brown leaves

There are numerous reasons why leaves can turn yellow or brown and drop off. Although it may seem obvious, first check whether it is simply a deciduous plant that naturally drops its leaves in the fall—you would be amazed how many people panic and forget this! Similarly, the leaves of Arbutus, Phillyrea, and Eriobotrya turn yellow and drop just before the new season's growth appears. This can be alarming to watch, but it should all last for only three to four weeks, and new growth soon fills in the empty spaces. Plants that have been newly transplanted can also suffer sudden leafdrop from the shock, but leaf loss is usually short-lived and foliage regrows quickly. Otherwise care issues could be to blame, for example, the plant may be suffering from severe underwatering, or lacking in nutrients and require extra feeding, or the soil could be too alkaline for the type of plant chosen, or it could be waterlogged.

Growth problems

If the plant is not flowering when it is supposed to, increase the plant's dose of potash in the spring. Ready-mixed tomato food is a good source of this. Pale and undersized leaves are most probably due to a nitrogen deficiency, which can be rectified by feeding the plant with something containing a high nitrogen content—for example, green manure or sulfate of ammonia, nitrochalk, or a dried blood mixture. The plant may also be in a restricted surrounding, such as a hanging basket, a window box, or a container that is too small for the plant. If there are leaves on your plant that are turning green when they should be variegated, cut out any shoots that are green and move the plant to a sunnier position.

Index of Plants

Acacia dealbata, see also
    Mimosa 19, 62
Acacia pravissima, see also
    Ovens Wattle 63
Acanthus mollis, see also
    Bear's Breeches 26, 107
African Lily, *Agapanthus
    africanus* 108
Agapanthus 16
Agapanthus africanus, see also
    African Lily 108
Agave americana + 'Variegata',
    see also The Century
    Plant 24, 92
Agave parryi 93
Agave salmiana var. 'Ferox' 94
Agaves 8, 10, 11, 13, 24, 52
Alexandrian Laurel, *Danae
    racemosa* 120
Albizia julibrissin, see also Silk
    Tree 19, 64
Albizia julibrissin 'Rosea', see
    also Silk Tree 64
Aloe aristata, see also Torch
    Plant 11, 95
Aloe striatula 96
Aralia elata, see also Japanese
    Angelica Tree 65
Araucaria araucana, see also
    Monkey Puzzle Tree 66
Arbutus 8, 10
Arbutus unedo, see also
    Strawberry tree 67
Arbutus x andrachnoides, see
    also Red-Barked
    Strawberry Tree 67
Arundinaria anceps 33
Arundo donax 25, 34
Aspidistra elatior, see also
    Cast-Iron Plant 109
Astelia chathamica, see also
    Silver Spear 110
Azara microphylla 68
Azorina vidalii 111

Baccharis 8
Baccharis patagonica, see also
    Magellan's Daisy Bush
    19, 112
Bamboos 8, 13, 16, 17
Bananas 8, 12, 16
Bear's Breeches, *Acanthus
    mollis* 26, 107
Beschorneria yuccoides 97
Billbergia nutans, see also
    Queen's Tears 113
Black Bamboo, *Phyllostachys
    nigra* 40
Blechnum chilense 44
Blechnum spicant, see also
    The Hard Fern 45
Blue Hesper Palm, *Brahea
    armata* 46
Brahea armata, see also Blue
    Hesper Palm 46

Bull Bay, *Magnolia grandiflora*
    27, 28, 79
Butia capitata, see also
    The Jelly Palm 47

Calla Lily, *Zantedeschia
    aethiopica*
    'Crowborough' 151
Canary Island Date Palm,
    Phoenix canariensis 50
Canna indica, see also Indian
    Shot Plant 16, 19, 26, 114
Canna iridiflora, see also Giant
    Canna Lily 115
Cannas 8, 16
Cardoon, *Cynara cardunculus*
    119
Carpobrotus edulis, see also
    Hottentot Fig 116
Cast-Iron Plant, *Aspidistra
    elatior* 109
Catalina Ironwood,
    *Lyonothamnus floribun-
    dus aspleniifolius* 78
Chamaerops humilis, see also
    Dwarf Fan Palm 10, 11,
    23, 43, 48
Chinese Privet, *Ligustrum
    lucidum* 77
Chusan Palm, *Trachycarpus
    fortunei* 10, 23, 48, 51
Clematis armandii 18, 52, 53
Clematis armandii 'Apple
    Blossom' 53
Colletia cruciata 98
Common yew, *Taxus baccata* 86
Cordyline australis 'Albertii',
    see also Cabbage Palm
    69
Cordyline australis, see also
    New Zealand Cabbage
    Palm 21, 22, 69
Cordylines 12, 23
Corokia x virgata 19, 117
Cortaderia selloana, see also
    Pampas Grass 25, 32, 35
Creeping Rosemary,
    Rosmarinus repens 10, 149
Crocosmia 'Lucifer', see also
    Montbretia 118
Cupressus sempervirens
    'Pyramidalis', see also
    Italian Cypress 70
Cupressus sempervirens, see
    also Italian Cypress
    70, 85
Cynara cardunculus, see also
    Cardoon 119
Cyperus alternifolius 36

Danae racemosa, see also
    Alexandrian Laurel 120
Daphne odora
    'Aureomarginata' 19, 121
Dasylirion 8, 11

Dasylirion acrotrichum 99
Dicksonia antarctica, see also
    Tasmanian Tree Fern 10,
    11, 21, 22, 49
Dicksonia squarrosa 22
Dracaena indivisa 69
Dwarf Fan Palm, *Chamaerops
    humilis* 10, 23, 43, 48

Echeveria glauca 11, 100
Echium pininiana 26, 122
Echiums 106
Ephedra, see also Mormon's Tea
    123
Eriobotrya japonica, see also
    The Loquat 71
Eryngium agavifolium 124
Eucalyptus 13, 19, 26
Eucalyptus aggregata, see also
    The Black Gum 72
Eucalyptus niphophila
    'Debeuzevillei', see also
    Jounama Snow Gum 73
Euonymus fortunei 'Kewensis'
    125
Euphorbia mellifera, see also
    Honey Spurge 26, 126
Euphorbia myrsinites, see also
    Myrtle Spurge 127
Euphorbia wulfenii, see also
    Spurge 128

Fascicularia bicolor, see also
    Firewheel 129
x *Fatshedera lizei* 54
Fatsia japonica, see also
    Japanese Fatsia 130
Fatsia japonica 'Moseri' 54
Fatsias 8, 9, 16, 106
Ferns 8, 9, 12, 43
Ficus carica, see also
    The Common Fig 19,
    74
Firewheel, *Fascicularia bicolor*
    129
Flannel Bush,
    Fremontodendron
    'California Glory' 131
Fremontodendron
    'California Glory', see
    also Flannel Bush 131

Gardenia 56
Genista aetnensis, see also
    Mount Etna Broom 75
Giant Canna Lily, *Canna
    iridiflora* 115
Giant Rhubarb, *Gunnera
    manicata* 132
Ginger lilies 106, 134, 135
Golden Bamboo, *Phyllostachys
    aurea* 38
Gunneras 8
Gunnera manicata, see also
    Giant Rhubarb 132

Hebe *parviflora angustifolia* 133
Hedera helix 'Hibernica' 54
Hedychium coccineum 'Tara',
    134
Hedychium forrestii, see also
    Ginger Lily 135
Hedychiums 16
Helleborus foetidus, see also
    Stinking Hellebore 136
Holboellia coriacea 55
Holboellia latifolia 18, 56
Holboellias 52
Holm Oak, *Quercus ilex* 8, 83, 89
Honey Spurge, *Euphorbia
    mellifera* 126
Hottentot Fig, *Carpobrotus
    edulis* 116
Hydrangea seemannii 18, 57

Indian Shot Plant, *Canna indica*
    16, 19, 26, 114
Iris confusa 137
Italian Cypress, *Cupressus
    sempervirens*
    'Pyramidalis' 70

Japanese Angelica Tree, *Aralia
    elata* 65
Japanese Banana, *Musa basjoo*
    20, 145
Japanese Fatsia, *Fatsia
    japonica* 130
Jasmine 52
Jounama Snow Gum,
    Eucalyptus niphophila
    'Debeuzevillei' 73

Kniphofia caulescens, see also
    Red Hot Poker 138

Lace-cap Hydrangea 57
Lampranthus spectabilis 140
Lardizabalaceae 55
Laurus nobilis angustifolia,
    see also Narrow-Leafed
    Bay 27, 76
Libertia formosa 11, 141
Ligustrum japonicum 77
Ligustrum lucidum, see also
    Chinese Privet 77
Lobelia tupa, see also Devil's
    Tobacco 142
*Lyonothamnus floribundus
    aspleniifolius*, see also
    Catalina Ironwood 78

Magellan's Daisy Bush,
    Baccharis patagonica
    19, 112
Magnolia grandiflora, see also
    Bull Bay 19, 27, 28, 79
Mahonias 106
Mahonia lomariifolia 143
Melianthus 106
Melianthus major 144

HarperCollins *practical gardener*

ARCHITECTURAL
PLANTS